# Introduction

*All you need to know about Protection* has been written as a reference book to help give you advice and to ensure that you have adequate financial protection for you, your family and any dependants. As a healthy working person with a good income, you may feel reasonably confident that you are able to provide for your family. However, your finances could be more precarious than you think. No matter what the current economic environment, adhering to a few sound and well-practiced strategies will help you to prepare for the future. While your individual situation will always have its unique qualities, our guide provides suggestions to consider as you review your family's long-term protection plans.

# Chapters

# **Chapter one**
## Life Insurance

It's understandable that we would rather not think of the time when we're no longer around. However, it's important to protect the things that really matter – like our loved ones, home and lifestyle – in case the unexpected happens.

### Financial safety net
We insure our cars, homes and even our mobile phones – so it goes without saying that we should also be insured for our full replacement value to ensure that our loved ones are financially catered for in the event of our premature death. Life insurance provides a safety net for your family and loved ones if you die, helping them cope financially during an otherwise difficult time.

We never know what life has in store for us, so it's important to get the right life insurance policy. A good place to start is asking yourself three questions: what do I need to protect? How much cover do I need? How long will I need cover for? This sum must take living costs into account, as well as any outstanding liabilities, such as a mortgage.

## Other living expenses

It may be the case that not everyone needs life insurance (also known as 'life cover' and 'death cover'). However, if your spouse and children, partner, or other relatives depend on your income to cover the mortgage or other living expenses, then the answer is 'yes'.

Life insurance makes sure they're taken care of financially if you die. So whether you're looking to provide a financial safety net for your loved ones, moving house or a first-time buyer looking to arrange your mortgage life insurance – or simply wanting to add some cover to what you've already got – you'll want to make sure you choose the right type of cover. That's why obtaining the right advice and knowing which products to choose – including the most suitable sum assured, premium, terms and payment provisions – is essential.

## Seriously under-insured

The appropriate level of life insurance will enable your dependants to cope financially in the event of your premature death. When you take out life insurance, you set the amount you want the policy to pay out should you die – this is called the 'sum assured'. Even if you consider that currently you have sufficient life assurance, you'll probably need more later on if your circumstances change. If you don't update your policy as key events happen throughout your life, you may risk being seriously under-insured.

## Own personal circumstances

As you reach different stages in your life, the need for protection will inevitably change. How much life insurance you need really depends on your circumstances, for example, whether you've got a mortgage, you're single or you have children. Before you compare life insurance, it's worth bearing in mind that the amount of cover you need will very much depend on your own personal circumstances, such as the needs of your family and dependants.

**Think about why you might need cover**

- What would happen if you died or were ill for a long time?
- Who are your financial dependants: your husband or wife, registered civil partner, children, brother, sister, or parents?
- What kind of financial support does your family have now?
- What kind of financial support will your family need in the future?
- What kind of costs will need to be covered such as household bills, living expenses, mortgage payments, education costs, debts or loans, or funeral costs?

There is no one-size-fits-all solution, and the amount of cover – as well as how long it lasts for – will vary from person to person.

**These are some events when you should consider reviewing your life insurance requirements:**

- Buying your first home with a partner
- Covering loans
- Getting married or entering into a registered civil partnership
- Starting a family
- Becoming a stay-at-home parent
- Having more children
- Moving to a bigger property
- Salary increases
- Changing your job
- Reaching retirement
- Relying on someone else to support you
- Personal guarantee for business loans.

**Individual lifestyle factors determine the cost**
The price you pay for a life insurance policy depends on a number of things. These include the amount of money you want to cover and

the length of the policy, but also your age, your health, your lifestyle, and whether you smoke.

## Replacing at least some of your income

If you have a spouse, partner or children, you should have sufficient protection to pay off your mortgage and any other liabilities. After that, you may need life insurance to replace at least some of your income. How much money a family needs will vary from household to household so, ultimately, it's up to you to decide how much money you would like to leave your family that would enable them to maintain their current standard of living.

## Two basic life insurance types

There are two basic types of life insurance, 'term life' and 'whole-of-life', but within those categories there are different variations.

The cheapest, simplest form of life insurance is term life insurance. It is straightforward protection, there is no investment element, and it pays out a lump sum if you die within a specified period. There are several types of term insurance.

The other type of protection available is a whole-of-life insurance policy, designed to provide you with cover throughout your entire lifetime. The policy only pays out once the policyholder dies, providing the policyholder's dependants with a lump sum, usually tax-free. Depending on the individual policy, policyholders may have to continue contributing right up until they die, or they may be able to stop paying in once they reach a stated age, even though the cover continues until they die.

Remove the burden of any debts Generally speaking, the amount of life insurance you may need should provide a lump sum that is sufficient to remove the burden of any debts and, ideally, leave enough over to invest in order to provide an income to support your dependants for the required period of time.

The first consideration is to clarify what you want the life insurance to protect. If you simply want to cover your mortgage, then an amount equal to the outstanding mortgage debt can achieve that.

**To prevent your family from being financially disadvantaged by your premature death and to provide enough financial support to maintain their current lifestyle, there are a few more variables you should consider:**

- What are your family expenses and how would they change if you died?
- How much would the family expenditure increase on requirements such as childcare if you were to die?
- How much would your family income drop if you were to die?
- How much cover do you receive from your employer or company pension scheme, and for how long?
- What existing policies do you have already, and how far do they go to meeting your needs?
- How long would your existing savings last?
- What state benefits are there that could provide extra support to meet your family's needs?
- How would the return of inflation to the economy affect the amount of your cover over time?

IF THE PLAN HAS NO INVESTMENT ELEMENT, IT WILL HAVE NO CASH IN VALUE AT ANY TIME AND WILL CEASE AT THE END OF THE TERM. IF PREMIUMS ARE NOT MAINTAINED, THEN COVER WILL LAPSE.

'Single life' policies cover just one person. A 'joint life' policy covers two people, and you will need to decide whether the policy pays out on the first or second death, as this will determine when the policy ends.

**When choosing between these options, think about:**

- Affordability – a joint life policy is usually more affordable than two separate single policies
- Cover needs – do you both have the same life insurance needs, or would separate policies with different levels of cover be more appropriate?
- Work benefits – if one of you has work 'death in service' benefit, you might only need one plan

# Chapter two
## Term life insurance

With a term life insurance policy, you choose the amount you want to be insured for and the period for which you want cover. This is the most basic type of life insurance. If you die within the term, the policy pays out to your beneficiaries. If you don't die during the term, the policy doesn't pay out, and the premiums you've paid are not returned to you.

There are two main types of term life insurance to consider: level-term and decreasing-term life insurance.

**Level-term life insurance policies**
A level-term policy pays out a lump sum if you die within the specified term. The amount you're covered for remains level throughout the term, hence the name. The monthly or annual premiums you pay usually stay the same, too.

Level-term policies can be a good option for family protection, where you want to leave a lump sum that your family can invest to live on after you've gone. It can also be a good option if you need a specified amount of cover for a certain length of time, for example, to cover an interest-only mortgage that's not covered by an endowment policy.

**Decreasing-term life insurance policies**
With a decreasing-term policy, the amount you're covered for decreases over the term of the policy. These policies are often used to cover a debt that reduces over time, such as repayment mortgages.

Premiums are usually cheaper than for level-term cover, as the amount insured reduces as time goes on. Decreasing-term assurance policies can also be used for Inheritance Tax planning purposes.

**Family income benefit policies**
Family income benefit life assurance is a type of decreasing term policy. Instead of a lump sum, though, it pays out a regular income to your beneficiaries until the policy's expiry date if you die.
You can arrange for the same amount of your take-home income to be paid out to your family if you die.

THE PLAN WILL HAVE NO CASH IN VALUE AT ANY TIME AND WILL CEASE AT THE END OF THE TERM. IF PREMIUMS ARE NOT MAINTAINED, THEN COVER WILL LAPSE.

# Chapter three
## Whole of Life Insurance

A whole-of-life insurance policy is designed to give you a specified amount of cover for the whole of your life, and it pays out when you die – whenever that is. Because it's guaranteed that you'll die at some point (and therefore that the policy will have to pay out), these policies are more expensive than term insurance policies, which only pay out if you die within a certain time frame.

**Paying Inheritance Tax**
Whole-of-life insurance policies can be a useful way to cover a future Inheritance Tax bill. If you think your estate will have to pay Inheritance Tax when you die, you could set up a whole-of-life insurance policy to cover the tax due, meaning that more is passed to your beneficiaries. To ensure the proceeds of the life insurance policy are not included in your estate, it is vital that the policy be written in an appropriate trust. This is a very complicated area of estate planning, and you should obtain professional advice.

A whole-of-life insurance policy has a double benefit: not only can the proceeds of the policy be written under trust so that they are outside your estate for Inheritance tax purposes, but the premium paid for the policy will reduce the value of your estate while you're alive, further reducing your estate's future Inheritance Tax bill.

**Different types of policy**

There are different types of whole-of-life insurance policy – some offer a set payout from the outset while others are linked to investments, and the payout will depend on performance. Investment-linked policies are either unit-linked policies linked to funds, or with-profits policies which offer bonuses.

Some whole-of-life policies require that premiums are paid all the way up to your death. Others become paid up at a certain age and waive premiums from that point onwards.

Whole-of-life policies (but not all) have an investment element and therefore a surrender value. If, however, you cancel the policy and cash it in, you will lose your cover. Where there is an investment element, your premiums are usually reviewed after ten years and then every five years.

Whole-of-life policies are also available without an investment element and with guaranteed or investment-linked premiums from some providers.

Reviews

The level of protection selected will normally be guaranteed for the first ten years, at which point it will be reviewed to see how much protection can be provided in the future. If the review shows that the same level of protection can be carried on, it will be guaranteed to the next review date.

**If the review reveals that the same level of protection can't continue, you'll have two choices:**

- Increase your payments
- Keep your payments the same and reduce your level of protection

## Maximum cover

Maximum cover offers a high initial level of cover for a lower premium until the first plan review, which is normally after ten years. The low premium is achieved because very little of your premium is kept back for investment, as most of it is used to pay for the life insurance.
After a review, you may have to increase your premiums significantly to keep the same level of cover, as this depends
on how well the cash in the investment reserve (underlying fund) has performed.

## Standard cover

This cover balances the level of life insurance with adequate investment to support the policy in later years. This should maintain the original premium throughout the life of the policy but is not guaranteed. However, it relies on the value of units invested in the underlying fund growing at a certain level each year. Increased charges or poor performance of the fund could mean you'll have to increase your monthly premium to keep the same level of cover.

THE VALUE OF INVESTMENTS AND THE INCOME FROM THEM MAY GO DOWN. YOU MAY NOT GET BACK THE ORIGINAL AMOUNT INVESTED.THE PLAN MAY HAVE NO CASH IN VALUE AT ANY TIME.

# Chapter four
## Critical illness Cover

We never think a critical illness is going to happen to us, especially when we feel fit and healthy, but it can and does. It can happen to anyone at any time, and it's easy to feel anxious about how we would cope. But if the worst does happen, it's important to make sure you're financially protected against the impact a critical illness could have on you and your family.

Critical illness cover could help to minimise the financial impact on you and your loved ones. For example, if you needed to give up work to recover, the money could be used to help fund the mortgage or rent, everyday bills, or even simple things like the weekly food shop – giving you and/or your family some peace of mind when you need it most.

## Surviving financial hardship

After surviving a critical illness, sufferers may not be able to return to work straight away (or ever) or may need home modifications or private therapeutic care. It is sad to contemplate a situation where someone survives a serious illness but fails to survive the ensuing financial hardship. Preparing for the worst is not something we want to think about when feeling fit and healthy, but you never know what life is going to throw at you next.

## Tax-free lump sum

Critical illness cover, either on its own or as part of a life assurance policy, is designed to pay you a tax-free lump sum on the diagnosis of certain specified life-threatening or debilitating (but not necessarily fatal) conditions, such as a heart attack, stroke, certain types/stages of cancer and multiple sclerosis. A more comprehensive policy will cover many more serious conditions, including loss of sight, permanent loss of hearing, and a total and permanent disability that stops you from working. Some policies also provide cover against the loss of limbs. However, not all conditions are necessarily covered, which is why you should always obtain professional advice.

## Much-needed financial support

If you are single with no dependants, critical illness cover can be used to pay off your mortgage, which means that you would have fewer bills or a lump sum to use if you became very unwell. And if you are part of a couple, it can provide much-needed financial support at a time of emotional stress.

## Exclusions and limitations

The illnesses covered are specified in the policy along with any exclusions and limitations, which may differ between insurers. Critical illness policies usually only pay out once, so they are not a replacement for income. Some policies offer combined life and critical illness cover. These pay out if you are diagnosed with a critical illness or you die, whichever happens first.

## Pre-existing conditions

If you already have an existing critical illness policy, you might find that by replacing a policy, you would lose some of the benefits if you have developed any illnesses since you took out the first policy. It is important to seek professional advice before considering replacing or switching your policy, as pre-existing conditions may not be covered under a new policy.

## Lifestyle changes
Some policies allow you to increase your cover, particularly after lifestyle changes such as marriage, moving home or having children. If you cannot increase the cover under your existing policy, you could consider taking out a new policy just to 'top up' your existing cover.

## Policy definition
A policy will provide cover only for conditions defined in the policy document. For a condition to be covered, your condition must meet the policy definition exactly. This can mean that some conditions, such as some forms of cancer, won't be covered if deemed insufficiently severe. Similarly, some conditions may not be covered if you suffer from them after reaching a certain age, for example, many policies will not cover Alzheimer's disease if diagnosed after the age of 60.

## Survival period
Very few policies will pay out as soon as you receive diagnosis of any of the conditions listed in the policy, and most pay out only after a 'survival period', which means that if you die within this period – even if you meet the definition of the critical illness given in the policy – the cover would not pay out.

## Range of factors
How much you pay for critical illness cover will depend on a range of factors including what sort of policy you have chosen, your age, the amount you want the policy to pay out, and whether or not you smoke.

'Permanent total disability' is usually included in the policy. Some insurers define permanent total disability as being unable to work as you normally would as a result of sickness, while others see it as being unable to independantly perform three or more 'Activities of Daily Living' as a result of sickness or accident.

**Activities of Daily Living include:**
- Bathing
- Dressing and undressing
- Eating
- Transferring from bed to chair and back again

**Make sure you're fully covered**

The good news is that medical advances mean more people than ever are surviving conditions that might have killed earlier generations. Critical illness cover can provide cash to allow you to pursue a less stressful lifestyle while you recover from illness, or you can use it for any other purpose. Don't leave it to chance – make sure you're fully covered.

IF THE POLICY HAS NO INVESTMENT ELEMENT, IT WILL HAVE NO CASH IN VALUE AT ANY TIME AND WILL CEASE AT THE END OF THE TERM. IF PREMIUMS ARE NOT MAINTAINED, THEN COVER WILL LAPSE. THE POLICY MAY NOT COVER ALL THE DEFINITIONS OF A CRITICAL ILLNESS. FOR DEFINITIONS, PLEASE REFER TO THE KEY FEATURES AND POLICY DOCUMENT.

# Chapter five
## Income protection insurance

No one likes to think that something bad will happen to them, but if you couldn't work due to a serious illness, how would you manage financially? Could you survive on savings or sick pay from work? If not, you may need some other way to keep paying the bills – and you might want to consider income protection insurance.

You might think this may not happen to you – and, of course, we hope it doesn't – but it's important to recognise that no one is immune to the risk of illness and accidents. Each year, close to a million people in the UK find themselves unable to work due to a serious illness or injury [1].

No one can guarantee that they will not be the victim of an unfortunate accident or be diagnosed with a serious illness. The bills won't stop arriving or the mortgage payments from being deducted from your bank account, so going without income protection insurance could be tempting fate.

## Providing monthly payments

Income protection insurance is a long-term insurance policy that provides a monthly payment if you can't work because you're ill or injured, and typically pays out until you can start working again, or until you retire, die or the end of the policy term – whichever is sooner.

**If you are unable to work, income protection insurance:**

- Replaces part of your income if you become ill or disabled
- Pays out until you can start working again, or until you retire, die or the end of the policy term – whichever is sooner
- Covers most illnesses that leave you unable to work, either in the short or long term (depending on the type of policy and its definition of incapacity)

There's a waiting period before the payments start, so you generally set payments to start after your sick pay ends, or after any other insurance stops covering you. The longer you wait, the lower the monthly payments.

You can claim as many times as you need to, while the policy is in force.

## Generous sickness benefits

Some people receive generous sickness benefits through their workplace, and these can extend right up until the date upon which they had intended to retire. However, some employees with long-term health problems could, on the other hand, find themselves having to rely on the state, which is likely to prove hard.

## Tax-free monthly income

Without a regular income, you may find it a struggle financially – even if you were ill for only a short period – and you could end up using your savings to pay the bills. In the event that you suffered from a serious illness, medical condition or accident, you could even find that you are never able to return to work. Few of us could cope financially if we were off work for more than six to nine months. Income protection insurance provides a tax-free monthly income for as long as required, up to retirement age, should you be unable to work due to long-term sickness or injury.

## Profiting from misfortune

Income protection insurance aims to put you back to the position you were in before you were unable to work. It does not allow you to make a profit out of your misfortune. So the maximum amount of income you can replace through insurance is broadly the after-tax earnings you have lost, less an adjustment for state benefits you can claim. This is typically translated into a percentage of your salary before tax, but the actual amount will depend on the company that provides your cover.

## Self-employment

If you are self-employed, then no work is also likely to mean no income. However, depending on what you do, you may have income coming in from earlier work, even if you are ill for several months. The self-employed can take out individual policies rather than business ones, but you need to ascertain on what basis the insurer will pay out. A typical basis for payment is your pre-tax share of the gross profit, after deduction of trading expenses, in the 12 months immediately prior to the date of your incapacity. Some policies operate an average over the last three years, as they understand that self-employed people often have a fluctuating income.

## Cost of cover

The cost of your cover will depend on your gender, occupation, age, state of health and whether or not you smoke. The 'occupation class' is used by insurers to decide whether a policyholder is able to return to work. If a policy will pay out only if a policyholder is unable to work in 'any occupation', it might not pay benefits for long – or indeed at all. The most comprehensive definitions are 'Own Occupation' or 'Suited Occupation'. 'Own Occupation' means you can make a claim if you are unable to perform your own job. However, being covered under 'Any Occupation' means that you have to be unable to perform any job, with equivalent earnings to the job you were doing before not taken into account.

**You can also usually choose for your cover to remain the same (level cover) or increase in line with inflation (inflation-linked cover):**

• **Level cover** – with this cover, if you made a claim, the monthly income would be fixed at the start of your plan and does not change in the future. You should remember that this means if inflation eventually starts to rise, the buying power of your monthly income payments may be reduced over time.

• **Inflation-linked cover** – with this cover, if you made a claim, the monthly income would go up in line with one of the inflation statistics like CPI or NAEI.

**When you take out cover, you usually have the choice of:**

• **Guaranteed premiums** – the premiums remain the same all the way throughout the term of your plan. If you have chosen inflation-linked cover, your premiums and cover will automatically go up each year in line with an inflation index.

• **Reviewable premiums** – this means the premiums you pay can increase or decrease in the future. The premiums will not typically increase or decrease for the first five years of your plan, but they may do so at any time after that. If your premiums do go up or down, they will not change again for the next 12 months.

## Making a claim

How long you have to wait after making a claim will depend on the waiting period. You can typically choose from between 1, 2, 3, 6, 12 or 24 months. The longer the waiting period you choose, the lower the premium for your cover will be – but you'll have to wait longer after you become unable to work before the payments from the policy are paid to you. Premiums must be paid for the entire term of the plan, including the waiting period.

## State benefits

Depending on your circumstances, it is possible that the payments from the plan may affect any state benefits due to you. This will depend on your individual situation and what state benefits you are claiming or intending to claim.

This market is subject to constant change in terms of the innovative new products that are being launched. If you are unsure whether any state benefits you are receiving will be affected, you should seek professional advice.

Source data:
[1] Association of British Insurers 2015

IF THE POLICY HAS NO INVESTMENT ELEMENT, IT WILL HAVE NO CASH IN VALUE AT ANY TIME AND WILL CEASE AT THE END OF THE TERM. IF PREMIUMS ARE NOT MAINTAINED, THEN COVER WILL LAPSE.

# Chapter six
## Private medical insurance

Nothing is more important to you than your health and the health of your family. If you or your loved ones were to experience worrying symptoms, private medical insurance can offer reassurance and control at a difficult time.

The National Health Service (NHS) was established in 1948 to provide healthcare to everyone in the UK regardless of wealth. Despite being one of the best healthcare systems in the world, the service is under increasing pressure from a growing, ageing population and being asked to make major efficiency savings.

**Concentrate on getting better sooner**
Diagnosis and treatment can be dealt with almost immediately, reducing the anxiety of the unknown and allowing you to concentrate on getting better sooner. With many health experts predicting that patients are set to experience poorer care and even longer waiting times, many people are turning to private health care for that extra peace of mind.

Private medical insurance (also known as 'health insurance') can supplement what's available on the NHS. If you don't already have it as part of your employee benefits package, and you can afford to pay the premiums, you might decide it's worth paying extra to have more choice over your care.

**Choice in the level of care**
Most UK residents are entitled to free healthcare from the NHS. One of the main reasons people take out private health insurance is to avoid long NHS waiting times. Health insurance pays all – or some – of your medical bills if you're treated privately. It gives you a choice in the level of care you get and how and when it is provided. You don't have to take out private medical insurance, but if you don't want to use the NHS, you might find it hard to pay for private treatment without insurance – especially for serious conditions.

Under private healthcare, it may also be possible to access the latest drugs and treatments, licensed by the National Institute of Health and Clinical Excellence (NICE), which aren't routinely available on the NHS (outpatient drugs are not covered).

**What does it cover?**
Like all insurance, the cover you receive from private medical insurance depends on the policy you buy. Basic private medical insurance usually covers the costs of most in-patient treatments (tests and surgery) and day-care surgery.

Some policies extend to out-patient treatments (such as specialists and consultants) and might pay you a small fixed amount for each night you spend in an NHS hospital.

You might also be able to choose a policy which covers mental health, depression and sports injuries, but these aren't always covered.

**There are two main types of private medical insurance policy:**

- Indemnity policies that meet the costs of having private medical treatment for an acute illness or injury on a short- term basis. This could include a private room in a hospital, surgeons' and other specialists' fees, outpatient treatment like physiotherapy, and day-care treatment including surgical and diagnostic procedures.

- Cash plan policies which provide a lump sum benefit payment in certain situations. Generally, the consumer will pay a monthly premium in return for cover, for up to 100% of costs for treatment like an inpatient stay in an NHS hospital, or dental or optical treatment. These may not be included under an indemnity policy.

**Both indemnity and cash-plan policies can have additional benefits. For example:**

- Cover for partners and/or children
- One-to-one telephone support for cancer and heart patients
- Patient health checks and helplines
- Access to complementary therapies and psychiatric treatment
- Dental and optical treatment
- Treatment at home for intravenous therapies like chemotherapy

Another variation is a six-week plan, which covers the costs of private medical treatment when NHS waiting times for that treatment are likely to be more than six weeks.

International private medical insurance policies (IPMI) provide medical treatment costs cover to expatriates living overseas.
Main benefits of private medical insurance are:

**Main benefits of private medical insurance are:**

- Shorter waiting times for treatment on the NHS
- Better facilities
- Faster diagnosis
- Choose from a range of private facilities
- Choose a convenient time for appointments and treatments

Nothing is more important to you than your health and the health of your family. If you or your loved ones were to experience worrying symptoms, private medical insurance offers reassurance and control at a difficult time.

THE PLAN WILL HAVE NO CASH IN VALUE AT ANY TIME AND WILL CEASE AT THE END OF THE TERM. IF PREMIUMS ARE NOT MAINTAINED, THEN COVER WILL LAPSE.

# Chapter seven
## Long-term care

With the UK's population ageing, more people will be living with long-term care needs. Oscar Wilde once said: 'The tragedy of old age is not that one is old, but that one is young.' But the good news of rising life expectancy also brings with it the challenge of how we fund our future care costs. The question is: who is responsible for looking after us if we need care in old age?

As we get older, it becomes more likely that we may need day-to-day help with activities such as washing and dressing or help with household activities such as cleaning and cooking. This type of support along with some types of medical care is what is called 'long-term care'.

**A good life in old age**
Demand for long-term care is expected to rise, thanks in part to our ageing population and increasing prevalence of long-term conditions such as dementia. This makes planning ahead essential, but when it comes to funding later life, it can get quite complicated, particularly since the costs depend on several unknowns including how long we are going to live.

The matter is further exacerbated because of how local authorities calculate whether a person needs financial assistance for the cost of residential care.

## Level of state support
The level of state support received can be different depending on whether you live in England, Wales, Scotland or Northern Ireland.

In England and Wales, for example, you can currently receive means-tested state assistance which depends on your savings and assets. For instance, if your savings and assets are above £23,250 in England, you will normally be expected to pay for the full cost of long-term care yourself.

Government state benefits can also provide some help but may not be enough or may not pay for the full cost of long-term care.

## Financial support assistance
Long-term care plans can provide the financial support you need if you have to pay for care assistance for yourself or a loved one. Additionally, some long-term care plans will cover the cost of assistance for those who need help to perform the basic activities of daily life such as getting out of bed, dressing, washing and going to the toilet.

You can receive long-term care in your own home or in residential or nursing homes.

Regardless of where you receive care, paying for care in old age is a growing issue.

## Planning for long-term care
There are a number of different ways to fund long-term care. These are some of the main options available for people needing to make provision.

## Immediate needs annuities
This annuity is a type of insurance policy that provides a regular income in exchange for an upfront lump sum investment. When used for long-term care, they provide a guaranteed income for life to pay for care costs in exchange for a one-off lump sum payment if you have care needs now. Income is tax-free if it is paid directly to the care provider.

## Enhanced annuities
You can use your pension to purchase an enhanced annuity (also known as an 'impaired life annuity') if you have a health problem, a long-term illness, if you are overweight or if you smoke. Annuity providers use full medical underwriting to determine a more accurate individual price. People with medical conditions including Parkinson's disease and multiple sclerosis, or those who have had a major organ transplant, are likely to be eligible for an enhanced annuity.

## Equity release schemes
If you need to fund your long-term care and have already paid off (or nearly paid off) your mortgage, an equity release scheme, if appropriate, could be one option to consider. It is important to obtain professional financial advice before committing to an equity release scheme. Your individual circumstances need to be assessed, and this is why financial advice is a must in the process and a regulatory requirement.

These schemes give you the ability to obtain a cash lump sum as a loan secured on your home. However, it's essential to make an informed decision and consider the options and alternatives available and any implications regarding state benefits, local authority support and tax obligations.

## Savings and investments
These two methods enable you to plan ahead and ensure your savings and assets are in place for your future care needs.
If you are already retired (or nearing retirement), you should ensure that your financial affairs are in order, for example, arranging or

updating your Will or a Power of Attorney. It also makes sense to ensure your savings, investments and other assets are in order in the event that you or your partner may need long-term care in the future.

If you are of working age, you are in the best position to plan for your future care needs. Accumulating wealth through investments or savings while you are earning will help with the potential costs of long-term care in later life.

**When planning for future care needs, what should you think about?**

- Who in your family may most need long-term care and for how long?
- Do you or another family member need to make long-term care provision now?
- Do you have sufficient money to pay for future long-term care fees?
- How long might you need to pay for a care fees plan?
- Is there the likelihood that home care or a nursing home may be required?
- What activities may you require help with, for example, help with dressing, using the toilet, feeding or mobility?
- Would your home require additional features such as a stair lift, an opening and closing bath or bath chair, and/or home help?

All in all, planning and timing is of utmost importance when it comes to funding for long-term care, and this is more the case now than ever.

EQUITY RELEASE MAY REQUIRE A LIFETIME MORTGAGE OR HOME REVERSION PLAN. TO UNDERSTAND THE FEATURES AND RISKS, ASK FOR A PERSONALISED ILLUSTRATION.

# Chapter eight
## Making a Will

We spend our lives working to provide for ourselves and our loved ones.

You may have a house or flat (in the UK or overseas), shares, savings and investments, as well as your personal possessions. All of these assets are your 'estate'. Making a Will ensures that when you die, your estate is shared according to your wishes.

Everyone should have a Will, but it is even more important if you have children, you own property or have savings, investments, insurance policies, or you own a business. Your Will lets you decide what happens to your money, property and possessions after your death.

If you make a Will, you can also make sure you don't pay more Inheritance Tax than you legally need to. It's an essential part of your financial planning. Not only does it set out your wishes, but die without a Will, and your estate will generally be divided according to the rules of intestacy – which may not reflect your wishes. Without one, the state directs who inherits – so your loved ones, relatives, friends and favorite charities may get nothing.

**Same-sex partners**
It is particularly important to make a Will if you are not married or are not in a registered civil partnership (a legal arrangement that gives same-sex partners the same status as a married couple). This is because the law does not automatically recognise cohabitants (partners who live together) as having the same rights as husbands, wives and civil partners. As a result, even if you've lived together for many years, your cohabitant may be left with nothing if you have not made a Will.

A Will is also vital if you have children or dependants who may not be able to care for themselves. Without a Will, there could be uncertainty about who will look after or provide for them if you die.
Peace of mind No one likes to think about it, but death is the one certainty that we all face. Planning ahead can give you the peace of mind that your loved ones can cope financially without you and, at a difficult time, helps remove the stress that monetary worries can bring. Planning your finances in advance should help you to ensure that, when you die, everything you own goes where you want it to. Making a Will is the first step in ensuring that your estate is shared out exactly as you want it to be.

If you leave everything to your spouse or registered civil partner, there'll be no Inheritance Tax to pay because they are classed as an exempt beneficiary. Or you may decide to use your tax-free allowance to give some of your estate to someone else or to a family trust. Scottish law on inheritance differs from English law.

**Good reasons to make a Will**
A Will sets out who is to benefit from your property and possessions (your estate) after your death.

**There are many reasons why you need to make a Will:**

- You can decide how your assets are shared – if you don't have a Will, the law says who gets what
- If you're an unmarried couple (whether or not it's a same-sex relationship), you can make sure your partner is provided for
- If you're divorced, you can decide whether to leave anything to your former partner
- You can make sure you don't pay more Inheritance Tax than necessary.
- You want to include a trust in your Will (perhaps to provide for young children or a disabled person, save tax, or simply protect your assets in some way after you die)
- Your permanent home is not in the UK or you are not a British citizen
- You live here but you have overseas property
- You own all or part of a business

Before you write a Will, it's a good idea to think about what you want included in it.

**You should consider:**

- How much money and what property and possessions you have
- Who you want to benefit from your Will
- Who should look after any children under 18 years of age.
- Who is going to sort out your estate and carry out your wishes after your death (your 'executor')

## Passing on your estate

An executor is the person responsible for passing on your estate. You can appoint an executor by naming them in your Will. The courts can also appoint other people to be responsible for doing this job. Once you've made your Will, it is important to keep it in a safe place and tell your executor, close friend or relative where it is.

## Review your Will

It is advisable to review your Will every five years and after any major change in your life, such as getting separated, married or divorced, having a child, or moving to a new house. Any change must be by 'codicil' (an addition, amendment or supplement to a Will) or by making a new Will.

# Chapter nine
## Power of Attorney

A Power of Attorney is a legal document that allows you to give someone else the legal authority to act on your behalf. There are several different types of Power of Attorney. A Lasting Power of Attorney (LPA) – previously called an 'Enduring Power of Attorney' – allows your attorneys to make decisions for you when you no longer wish to, or when you lack the mental capacity to do so.

When making an LPA, you are permitting someone to act on your behalf when you are no longer mentally capable of making decisions on your behalf.

**Different types of LPA**

**Health and Welfare** – this covers health and care decisions and can only be used once you have lost mental capacity.

**A LPA can generally make decisions about things such as:**

- Where you should live
- Your medical care
- What you should eat
- Who you should have contact with
- What kind of social activities you should take part in

You can also give special permission for your attorney to make decisions about life-saving treatment.

**Property and Financial Affairs** – an LPA for financial decisions can be used while you still have mental capacity, or you can state that you only want it to come into force if you lose capacity.

**An LPA for financial decisions can cover things such as:**

- Buying and selling property
- Paying the mortgage
- Investing money
- Paying bills
- Arranging repairs to property

You can restrict the types of decisions your attorney can make, or you can let them make all decisions on your behalf.

If you're setting up an LPA for financial decisions, your attorney must keep accounts and make sure their money is kept separate from yours. You can ask for regular details of how much is spent and how much money you have. This offers you an extra layer of protection. These details can be sent to your solicitor or a family member if you lose capacity.

## Making decisions

A property and financial affairs LPA allows your attorneys to make decisions regarding your finances. This could include decisions about paying bills, operating your bank accounts or even selling your home.

A health and welfare LPA allows your attorneys to make decisions for things such as medical treatment, accepting or refusing types of health care, and whether or not you continue to live in your own home. You can also give your attorneys the power to make decisions about life-sustaining treatment for you. Your attorneys can be the same as those appointed under the property and financial affairs LPA.

## Financial affairs

If you decide not to make an LPA and subsequently lack the mental capacity to understand the nature and effect of the document, you may no longer be able to create an LPA. In those circumstances, if you are no longer mentally capable of dealing with your financial affairs, someone will have to make an application to the Court of Protection to be appointed as what is called your 'deputy'. This process applies even if the person incapacitated is your spouse or registered civil partner.

To avoid the court making decisions on your behalf, it is therefore beneficial to create an LPA because it allows you to decide in advance:

- The decisions you want to be made on your behalf if you lose the capacity to make them yourself
- The people you want to make these decisions
- How you want the people to make these decisions

## Who will have the authority?

If you're married or in a registered civil partnership, you may have assumed that your spouse would automatically be able to deal with your bank account and pensions and make decisions about your healthcare if you lose the ability to do so. This is not the case. Without an LPA, they won't have the authority.

## Enduring Power of Attorney

Enduring Powers of Attorney (EPA) were replaced by LPAs in October 2007. However, if you made and signed an EPA before 1 October 2007, it should still be valid.

You might already be using an EPA without having registered it so that someone can act on your behalf. This is fine until you become unable to make your own decisions relating to financial and property matters. Once this happens, your attorney must register your EPA before they can take any further action on your behalf.

An EPA only covers decisions about your property and financial affairs; an attorney doesn't have power under an EPA to make decisions about your health and care. You might want to consider setting up an LPA for health and care decisions to work alongside the existing EPA.

# Chapter ten
## Inheritance tax

There are many things to consider when looking to protect your family and your home. Protecting your estate is ultimately about securing more of your wealth for your loved ones and planning for what will happen after your death to make the lives of your loved ones much easier. It's not nice to think about, but it means that your loved ones can carry out your wishes and be protected from Inheritance Tax.

If you don't make the right financial arrangements, your family could have to foot a hefty Inheritance Tax bill in the event of your premature death. Passing assets efficiently to the next generation remains a primary objective for many who have spent a lifetime accumulating their wealth. Providing funds for family members or a charitable interest is also an important way to see the benefit of your wealth during your lifetime as well as leaving a legacy.

## Peace of mind

Making sure that you've made plans for after you're gone will give you peace of mind. It's not nice to think about, but it means that your loved ones can carry out your wishes and be protected from Inheritance Tax.

You don't have to be wealthy for your estate to be liable for Inheritance Tax, and it isn't something that is paid only on death, as it may also have to be paid on gifts made during someone's lifetime. The rate of Inheritance Tax on death is 40% and on chargeable lifetime transfers at 20%.

Your estate will be liable if it is valued over the current Inheritance Tax threshold on your death. The Inheritance Tax threshold, or Nil Rate Band (NRB), is currently at £325,000 (2019/20). This amount has been frozen at £325,000 since 2009, and HM Revenue & Customs have confirmed that it will remain frozen at this level up to and including the 2020/21 tax year.

There is no accounting for inflation, and therefore the effect of this freezing of the NRB is such that increasingly more estates may have an Inheritance Tax liability.

## Residence nil rate band

HM Revenue & Customs have accepted that an increasing number of individuals with relatively modest assets – and particularly where they relate mainly to the value of the house – should not be subject to Inheritance Tax. From 6 April 2017, they have introduced an additional NRB for deaths which occur on or after 6 April 2017 where the main residence passes to direct descendants. The amount of the relief is being phased in over four years starting at £100,000 in the first year and rising to £175,000 for 2020/21.

This is available to each individual, and therefore for a married couple this is potentially £350,000. On the second death of the couple, there will potentially be in effect a total NRB band of £1 million from 2020/21.

The additional NRB can only be used in respect of one residential property which does not have to be the main family home but must at some point have been a residence of the deceased.

The residence NRB may also be available where an individual downsized or ceased to own a home on or after 8 July 2015 where assets of an equivalent value, up to the value of the residence NRB, are passed on death to direct descendants. How this applies will be subject to conditions and depends on the total value of the estate and the home.

Any unused proportion of the NRB or residence NRB belonging to the first spouse or registered civil partner to die can be passed to the surviving spouse or registered civil partner.

## Exemptions
Moving ownership of assets to your spouse or registered civil partner may help reduce the Inheritance Tax liability on your estate. However, don't forget that this can cause an increased Inheritance Tax liability when they die. There are also exemptions if you make a donation to a charity.

## Making gifts
If you can afford to make gifts during your lifetime, this will also reduce the value of your estate, and so your ultimate Inheritance Tax liability. You can make a gift of up to £3,000 a year without any Inheritance Tax liability, and if you don't use this whole allowance, it can be carried forward to the next tax year. You can also give gifts of up to £250 a year to any number of people with no IHT liability.

There are two types of gift which currently have tax implications. The first is Chargeable Lifetime Transfers (CLTs). The most common chargeable transfers are lifetime gifts into Discretionary Trusts. A transfer will be charged if (together with any chargeable transfers made in the previous seven years) it exceeds the Inheritance Tax NRB (currently £325,000). Tax is paid at 20% on excess over the NRB.

The other type of gift to be aware of is Potentially Exempt Transfers (PETs). Gifts between individuals or into a bare trust arrangement are examples of PETs. These gifts are free from Inheritance Tax provided you survive more than seven years beyond the date of the gift. The other area to be aware of is that if you are making a gift but try to reserve any of the benefit for yourself.

For example, retaining dividend income from shares you have gifted, or living rent-free in a property you have. The gift will not be effective for Inheritance Tax planning purposes.

**Life insurance policy**
Taking out a life insurance policy written under an appropriate trust could be used towards paying any Inheritance Tax liability. Under normal circumstances, the payout from a life insurance policy will form part of your legal estate and may therefore be subject to Inheritance Tax. By writing a life-insurance policy in an appropriate trust, the proceeds from the policy can be paid directly to the beneficiaries rather than to your legal estate and will therefore not be taken into account when Inheritance Tax is calculated. It also means payment to your beneficiaries will probably be quicker, as the money will not go through probate.

INFORMATION IS BASED ON OUR CURRENT UNDERSTANDING OF TAXATION LEGISLATION AND REGULATIONS. ANY LEVELS AND BASES OF, AND RELIEFS FROM TAXATION, ARE SUBJECT TO CHANGE

# Chapter eleven
## Setting up a trust

The structures into which you can transfer your assets can have lasting consequences for you and your family, and it is crucial that you choose the right ones. The right structures can protect assets and give your family lasting benefits. A trust can be used to reduce how much Inheritance Tax your estate will have to pay on your death.

**Legal arrangement**
A trust, in principle, is a very simple concept. It is a legal arrangement where the ownership of someone's assets (such as property, shares or cash) is transferred to someone else (usually a small group of people or a trust company) to manage and use to benefit a third person (or group of people). Broadly speaking, there are three types of trust to choose from: a Discretionary Trust, Life Interest Trust and Bare Trust. An appropriate trust can be used to reduce how much Inheritance Tax your estate will have to pay on your death.

## Bare (Absolute) Trusts

The beneficiaries are entitled to a specific share of the trust, which can't be changed once the trust has been established. The settlor (the person who puts the assets in trust) decides on the beneficiaries and shares at outset. This is a simple and straightforward trust – the trustees invest the trust fund for the beneficiaries but don't have the power to change the beneficiaries interests decided on by the settlor at outset. This trust offers the potential Income and Capital Gains Tax benefits, particularly for minor beneficiaries. For minor beneficiaries, if funds are provided by the parents, the income can be taxed on the parents if it exceeds £100pa (parental settlement rules).

## Life Interest Trusts

Typically, one beneficiary will be entitled to the income from the trust fund whilst alive, with capital going to another (or other beneficiaries) on that beneficiary's death. This is often used in Will planning to provide security for a surviving spouse, with the capital preserved for children. This can also be used to pass income from an asset onto a beneficiary without losing control of the capital. This can be particularly attractive in second marriage situations when the children are from an earlier marriage.

## Discretionary (Flexible) Trusts

The settlor decides who can potentially benefit from the trust, but the trustees are then able to use their discretion to determine who, when and in what amounts beneficiaries do actually benefit. This provides maximum flexibility compared to the other trust types and for this reason is often referred to as a 'Flexible Trust'.

TAX TREATMENT DEPENDS ON INDIVIDUAL CIRCUMSTANCES AND MAY BE SUBJECT TO CHANGE IN THE FUTURE. THE INFORMATION GIVEN IS NOT INTENDED TO PROVIDE LEGAL, TAX OR FINANCIAL ADVICE.

# Chapter twelve
## Family Succession Planning

Family succession planning is a journey that should commence the day you start your business, but often only commences with a trigger – in other words, something that has initiated the decision to start the succession process. It may be one of the most challenging experiences facing any business leader, especially an entrepreneurial business person who has built a family business from scratch, so it is crucial to get right.

For a family business, transition is a once-in-a-lifetime decision. Perhaps no challenge has as much potential to exacerbate the special stresses – or, conversely, highlight the special advantages – of operating a family business.

### PROSPERITY FOR GENERATIONS TO COME
A good succession plan can be the first step in maintaining the strength of an enterprise and the family's prosperity for generations to come. Discussing how a family business should continue beyond

the career, or even the life, of the founder can be difficult, as it often crosses business and personal spheres. Issues around succession planning make up four of the top ten worries keeping family business owners awake at night, according to research from Close Brothers Asset Management (CBAM), conducted by Family Business United. Families who are in business must give their attention to the organisational needs of not only their business but also that of their family and, most importantly, those areas where business and family intersect. Often family and business are so closely interwoven that it is almost impossible for the family to come together without bringing the business with them. This is not always a good thing, and family meetings are not necessarily the ideal setting to consider and discuss business.

## EVEN HARDER PROCESS

The challenges faced by the second and third generations are substantially different from that faced by the first generation. Also, given that the first generation is often highly entrepreneurial, they often tend to overlook succession planning until the last moment. This makes the process even harder.

A survey of family businesses found that management succession planning was a worry for 39% of business owners, while 35% cited engaging and developing the next generation as a concern. Ownership succession and developing responsible future owners was stated as a worry by more than a third (34%) of business owners. The same number also highlighted identifying and maintaining family values as an ongoing concern.

## PLANNING FOR LATER LIFE

The day-to-day running of the business came in as the top worry for family business owners, with 40% saying that continuing to develop and remain a profitable business was a key concern. Personal finances also stood out, with worries about planning for later life highlighted by 38% of owners.

Outside of family businesses' immediate control, four in ten (39%) business owners said red tape, regulation and legislation was a worry. Family businesses employ almost 12 million people [1] and turn over an estimated £1.3 trillion each year, which is over a third of the turnover of the private sector[2].

## FAMILY OWNED SMALL BUSINESSES

UK SMEs face a multitude of challenges, and family owned small businesses can have an especially hard time navigating regulation and adapting to changing policy while remaining loyal to their unique set of family values. Beyond that, all this must be done while running a profitable business.

Succession planning is naturally a significant concern for family businesses and requires careful consideration. Not only must owners consider developing their replacement and ensure family values are adhered to, but they must also plan for their own retirement. Taking advice early and developing a personal financial plan is crucial to alleviating anxiety and meeting long-term goals.

## TOP TEN WORRIES KEEPING FAMILY BUSINESS OWNERS AWAKE AT NIGHT

1. Continuing to develop and remain a profitable business
2. Management succession planning
3. Red tape, regulation and legislation
4. Planning for later life
5. Engaging and developing the next generation
6. Ownership succession and developing responsible future owners
7. Identifying and maintaining family values
8. Extracting value from the business
9. Taxation
10. Developing effective marketing, social media and PR strategies

## LOOKING TO DEVELOP A SUSTAINABLE FAMILY ORGANISATION FOR YEARS TO COME?

Succession planning can be a complex process, although breaking it down into its component parts makes developing one a whole lot easier. Handing a family business to the next generation is a major process – from selecting and developing the successors to protecting the brand reputation and retaining knowledge – but the effort is crucial to developing a sustainable organisation for years to come. To discuss your requirements, please contact us for further information.

Source data:
The research was commissioned by Close Brothers Asset Management and conducted by Family Business United in Q4 2015. 173 family businesses were surveyed across the UK. [1] Figures from Oxford Economics for the Institute of Family Business (IFB) [2]Figures from research conducted by Family Business United (2015)

# Chapter thirteen
## Shareholder and partnership protection

If your business partner or a shareholder died or became critically ill, have you ever thought what the impact could be?

The loss of a business partner or a shareholder can have a major impact on the success of any business. But it's not just about the loss of profits the business could suffer. Who would take their place? Not only in performing their day-to-day duties, but also in making decisions of how your business is run in the future.

**NO KNOWLEDGE OF THE BUSINESS**

You could even be forced to work with a member of their family who has no knowledge of the business and isn't really that interested in it. That family member would now have the same say as your partner before they died. This could be very disruptive or totally unacceptable to the other partner/shareholders. The family may even want to sell their share of the business, which could be bought by a competitor or other unsuitable buyer.

Also, if your shareholding director or partner becomes critically ill, this could lead to uncertainty for the business. Would they be able to return to work? Would they even want to? Would they want to sell their shares following a health scare?

## WHEN THE UNEXPECTED HAPPENS

Unlike the other forms of business protection, shareholder or partnership protection covers individuals rather than the company. It can help solve many of the problems that could arise when the unexpected happens.

The protection needs of shareholders and partners are broadly similar. This protection gives you and your partners the security of being able to keep the ownership of the business in the hands of the people who have built it by enabling you to 'buy out' the share of a business colleague who has died or become too ill to carry on working at a fair price.

## ENSURE CONTROL OF THE COMPANY

It can also form part of an arrangement that is designed to ensure that control of the company stays in the hands of the current owners, and that the family that inherits the shares receives their full value. If a company's Articles of Association includes a pre-emption clause, the remaining shareholders have an automatic right to buy the shares of a partner who dies or leaves due to illness.

If a partnership has not drawn up a partnership agreement, under current law the partnership will end on the death of any of the partners. With suitable cover and a suitable arrangement in place, the remaining owners would not have the issue of raising capital to buy out a business owner who is critically ill, or the heirs of a business owner who has died and allows them to keep control of the business.

## ESTABLISH THE SUMS ASSURED NEEDED

Typically, each individual business owner needs to take out a separate plan, written under a business assurance trust. The business owners must decide between life cover and critical illness cover, or a combination of the two. The policy can be a fixed or whole life term, depending on the business owner's specific needs.

The amount of cover should reflect the value of each owner's full share in the business. One way of measuring this is as a proportion of the capital value of the business, plus the goodwill included in the accounts, any undistributed profits, and the individual's loan or partnership account. The value of the business should be assessed professionally to establish the sums assured needed, and underwriters may ask to see a copy of the valuation.

## IMPORTANCE OF OBTAINING PROFESSIONAL ADVICE

Each person should be covered for the full value of their share of the business. The value of each share should be reviewed regularly to ensure that the cover remains adequate, as the value of a company can change over time. It can therefore be useful for the policy to have the flexibility to accommodate this, both through annual inflation-proofing increases and through large single increases. A valuable feature can be the ability to increase without giving further health evidence.

How the business protection is established and what it is designed to do may impact the taxation of any benefits received or premiums paid. There should be a business agreement in place detailing how the funds would be used after a claim, for example, a cross option or single option agreement. Each company's circumstances are different – and whichever route is chosen, it is important that you obtain professional advice to ensure the most appropriate arrangements are put in place.

# Chapter fourteen
## Protecting yourself from scams

Fraudsters are getting more deceitful and ever more successful. Pension and investment scams are on the increase in the UK. Everyday fraudsters are using sophisticated ways to part savers from their money, and the Internet and advances in digital communications mean these kinds of scams are getting more common and harder to identify. A lifetime's savings can be lost in moments.

Nearly one in ten over-55s fear they have been targeted by suspected scammers since the launch of pension freedoms, new research [1] shows.

## Tactics commonly used to defraud
The study found 9% of over-55s say they have been approached about their pension funds by people they now believe to be scammers since the rules came into effect from April 2015. Offers to unlock or transfer funds are tactics commonly used to defraud people of their retirement savings.

One in three (33%) over-55s say the risk of being defrauded of their savings is a major concern following pension freedoms. However, nearly half (49%) of those approached say they did not report their concerns because they did not know how to or were unaware of who they could report the scammers to.

## Reporting suspected scammers to authorities
Most recent pension fraud data [2] from ActionFraud, the national fraud and cybercrime reporting service, shows 991 cases have been reported since the launch of pension freedoms involving losses of more than £22.687 million

## Alternative investments such as wine offered
The research found fewer than one in five (18%) of those approached by suspected scammers had reported their fears to authorities. Nearly half (47%) said the approaches involved offers to unlock pension funds or access money early, and 44% said they involved transferring pensions.

About 28% of those targeted by suspected fraudsters were offered alternative investments such as wine, and 20% say they were offered overseas investments, while 13% say scammers had suggested investing in crypto currencies. Around 6% believe they have been victims of fraud.

## Safeguarding hard-earned retirement savings

Pension freedoms, though enormously popular with consumers, have created a potentially lucrative opportunity for fraudsters, and people need to be vigilant to safeguard their hard-earned retirement savings.

If it sounds too good to be true, then it usually is, and people should be sceptical of investments that are offering unusually high rates of return or which invest in unorthodox products which may be difficult to understand. If in any doubt, seeking professional financial advice from a regulated adviser will help ensure you don't get caught out.

Source data:
The Financial Services Compensation Scheme.

**Some scammers have very convincing websites and other online presence, which make them look like a legitimate company. Always check with the FCA to make sure they're registered**

### Top five financial scams to look out for in the UK

### 1. Boiler-room schemes

These scams promise investors impressive returns, but they deliver nothing apart from a great big loss. More than 5,000 investors lost a combined £1.73 billion through boiler-room schemes reported to the Action Fraud crime-prevention centre in 2014. Victims will receive a telephone call out of the blue and be offered an investment opportunity with sky-high returns of as much as 40%. You will most likely be told that you must act fast and asked to transfer your money straight away. It's common for victims to part with tens of thousands of pounds. Boiler rooms are not authorised by the Financial Conduct Authority (FCA). This means that if you hand over your cash, it might be the last you will see of it.

### Take Action

Check the FCA status of any firm you intend to deal with for investments. Call 0800 1116768 or go to www.fca.org.uk/register.

## 2. Phishing/Smishing

The most common scams come from fraudsters posing as someone official, such as your bank or building society. Typically, you receive an email or text asking you to click a link and verify login, account and password details. The communication received is from a fraudster who will be able to read the information you type in, should you fall for their trick. This information is then used to raid your account. If you lose money this way, you won't get it back.

## Take Action

Your bank will never ask you to disclose full security and password details, so alarm bells should ring. If in doubt, call your bank and ask them if they have tried to contact you.

## 3. Pension liberation

Scammers are bombarding people aged 55 and over with bogus investment opportunities to try to get hold of their pension savings.
One of the most common scams since the pension freedoms were announced involves alleged investment opportunities abroad
Low interest rates are tempting some people to take extra risks, so they are vulnerable to such fake investments. Fraudsters can approach you by post, email or telephone.

## Take Action

If you're offered a 'must-have' investment or a free pension 'review' out of the blue, be wary. Also, be concerned if you're warned that the deal is limited, and you must act now. Choosing the right retirement income product is a big decision and shouldn't be done quickly or under pressure.

Consult a registered professional financial adviser. If you think that you may have been made a fraudulent offer, contact Action Fraud on 0300 1232040 or visit the FCA's Scam Smart site to see if the investment you've been offered is on their warning list:
http://scamsmart.fca.org.uk/warninglist.

## 4. Homebuying fraud

This con intercepts cash transferred as a home deposit to a solicitor in the lead-up to exchange and completion. It's all done via the Internet where a computer hacker monitors emails sent between a solicitor and client. When a bank transfer is about to be made, the fraudster emails the homebuyer pretending to be the solicitor, telling them the details of the law firm's bank account have changed. The unsuspecting homebuyer sends their cash to the new account, where it is withdrawn by the fraudsters.

### Take Action

If you're buying a property, watch for any emails about payments, such as a change in bank details at the last minute. Many victims are told that the account is being 'audited', and so another one must be used. Ring your solicitor if you're in any doubt.

## 5. Freebie scams

Seemingly free trial offers for products are duping consumers out of millions of pounds a year. To get the freebies, you need to enter your card details – although told you won't be charged for the introductory period. In fact, you are often signing up to an expensive monthly subscription that is very difficult to get out of. Once this type of billing is approved – known as 'continuous payment authorisation' – up to £100 a month can be taken without any further contact.

### Take Action

Report such free trial offers to The Advertising Standards Authority contact 020 7492 2222 or to make a complaint visit https://www.asa.org. uk/make-a-complaint.html

PROVIDING OPPORTUNITIES FOR THE FUTURE

# The Foundation provides local financial resources in the form of gifts to youth clubs, schools and organisations.

We fund structured, purposeful projects and ventures in and around Shropshire and Cheshire, giving youths the opportunity of reaching their full potential.

## Work we have supported for the community

We have supported many projects that have positively impacted many groups of people within the community we have donated to date over £25,000 to:

Team funding, Sports equipment and kits, Charity fundraising activities, School projects, Guides, Scouts and Youth Clubs.

Please donate now and help us continue with our good work...

Every pound you put in is a pound that is given out.

All running costs are covered.

# Glossary of Financial Terms

*A*

*Alpha*

Alpha is a measure of a fund's over or under performance compared to its benchmark. It represents the return of the fund when the benchmark is assumed to have a return of zero. It shows the extra value that the manager's activities seem to have contributed. If the Alpha is 5, the fund has outperformed its benchmark by 5% and the greater the Alpha, the greater the out performance.

*Alternative Assets*

Includes private real estate, public real estate, venture capital, non-venture private equity, hedge funds, distressed securities, oil and gas partnerships, event arbitrage, general arbitrage, managed funds, commodities, timber and other.

*American Stock Exchange*

AMEX is the second-largest stock exchange in the U.S., after the New York Stock Exchange (NYSE). In general, the listing rules are a little more lenient than those of the NYSE, and thus the AMEX has a larger representation of stocks and bonds issued by smaller companies than the NYSE. Some index options and interest rate options trading also occurs on the AMEX. The AMEX started as an alternative to the NYSE. It originated when brokers began meeting on the curb outside the NYSE in order to trade stocks that failed to meet the Big Board's stringent listing requirements, but the AMEX now has its own trading floor. In 1998, the parent company of the NASDAQ purchased the AMEX and combined their markets, although the two continue to operate separately. Also called The Curb.

*Annual Rate of Return*

There are several ways of calculating this. The most commonly used methodologies reflect the compounding effect of each period's increase or decrease from the previous period.

## Annual Percentage Rate (APR)

The APR is designed to measure the "true cost of a loan". The aim is to create a level playing field for lenders preventing them from advertising a low rate and hiding fees. In the case of a mortgage the APR should reflect the yearly cost of a mortgage, including interest, mortgage insurance, and the origination fee, expressed as a percentage.

## Annual Premium Equivalent

Calculated as regular premiums plus 10% of single premiums.

## Arbitrage

A financial transaction or strategy that seeks to profit from a price differential perceived with respect to related or correlated instruments in different markets. Typically involves the simultaneous purchase of an instrument in one market and the sale of the same or related instrument in another market.

## Asset Allocation

Apportioning of investment funds among categories of assets such as cash equivalents, stock, fixed-income investments, alternative investments such as hedge funds and managed futures funds, and tangible assets like real estate, precious metals and collectibles.

## Average Monthly Gain

The average of all the profitable months of the fund.

## Average Monthly Loss

The average of all the negative months of the fund.

## Average Monthly Return

The average of all the monthly performance numbers of the fund.

# B

## Basis Point
A basis point is one one-hundredth of a percent i.e. 50 basis points or "bps" is 0.5%.

## Bear / Bear Market
Bear is a term describing an investor who thinks that a market will decline. The term also refers to a short position held by a market maker. A Bear Market is a market where prices are falling over an extended period.

## Bellwether
A stock or bond that is widely believed to be an indicator of the overall market's condition. Also known as Barometer stock.

## Beta
Beta is a measure of a fund's volatility compared to its benchmark, or how sensitive it is to market movements. A fund with a Beta close to 1 means that the fund will move generally in line with the benchmark. Higher than 1 and the fund is more volatile than the benchmark, so that with a Beta of 1.5, say, the fund will be expected to rise or fall 1.5 points for every 1 point of benchmark movement. If this Beta is an advantage in a rising market – a 15% gain for every 10% rise in the benchmark –the reverse is true when markets fall. This is when managers will look for Betas below 1, so that in a down market the fund will not perform as badly as its benchmark.

## Bid Price
The price at which an investor may sell units of a fund back to the fund manager. It is also the price at which a market maker will buy shares.

## Blue Chips
Large, continuously well performing stock, presumed to be among the safer investments on an exchange.

## Bond

A debt investment, with which the investor loans money to an entity (company or Government) that borrows the funds for a defined period of time at a specified interest rate. The indebted entity issues investors a certificate, or bond, that states the interest rate (coupon rate) that will be paid and when the loaned funds are to be returned (maturity date). Interest on bonds is usually paid every six-months.

### Bond Rating Codes

| Rating | S&P | Moody's |
|---|---|---|
| Highest quality | AAA | Aaa |
| High quality | AA | Aa |
| Upper medium quality | A | A |
| Medium grade | BBB | Baa |
| Somewhat speculative | BB | Ba |
| Low grade, speculative | B | B |
| Low grade, default possible | CCC | Caa |
| Low grade, partial recovery possible | CC | Ca |
| Default, recovery unlikely | C | C |

## Bottom up Investing

An approach to investing which seeks to identify well performing individual securities before considering the impact of economic trends.

## BRIC

A term used to refer to the combination of Brazil, Russia, India and China. General consensus is that the term was first prominently used in a thesis of the Goldman Sachs Investment Bank. The main point of this 2003 paper was to argue that the economies of the BRICs are rapidly developing and by the year 2050 will eclipse most of the current richest countries of the world. Due to the popularity of the Goldman Sachs thesis, "BRIC" and "BRIMC" (M for Mexico), these terms are also extended to "BRICS" (S for South Africa) and "BRICKET" (including Eastern Europe and Turkey) and have become more generic terms to refer to these emerging markets.

## Bull / Bull Market

An investor who believes that the market is likely to rise. A Bull Market is a market where prices are rising over an extended period.

## Bulldog Bond

A sterling denominated bond that is issued in London by a company that is not British. These sterling bonds are referred to as bulldog bonds as the bulldog is a national symbol of England.

# C

## Child Trust Fund

A Child Trust Fund is a savings and investment account for children. Children born on or after 1st September 2002 will receive a £250 voucher to start their account. The account belongs to the child and can't be touched until they turn 18, so that children have some money behind them to start their adult life. Payments or contributions can be made up to a maximum of £1,200 per 12 month period (starting on the birthday of the child), excluding the voucher amount. Interest and capital growth will be earned tax-free. Additional deposits can be made by parents, grandparents or anyone else.

## Closed-end Fund

Type of fund that has a fixed number of shares or units. Unlike open-ended mutual funds, closed-end funds do not stand ready to issue and redeem shares on a continuous basis.

## Collar

A contract that protects the holder from a rise or fall in interest rates or some other underlying security above or below certain fixed points. The contract offers the investor protection from interest rate moves outside of an expected range.

## Constant Proportion Portfolio Insurance CPPI

Strategy that basically buys shares as they rise and sells shares as they fall. To implement a CPPI strategy, the investor selects a floor below which the portfolio value is not allowed to fall. The floor increases in value at the rate of return on cash. If you think of the difference between the assets and floor as a "cushion", then the

CPPI decision rule is to simply keep the exposure to shares a constant multiple of the cushion.

## Consumer Discretionary Sector

The array of businesses included in the Consumer Discretionary Sector are categorized into five industry groups. They are: Automobiles and Components; Consumer Durables and Apparel; Hotels, Restaurants and Leisure; Media; and Retailing.

## Consumer Staples

The industries that manufacture and sell food/beverages, tobacco, prescription drugs and household products. Proctor and Gamble would be considered a consumer staple company because many of its products are household and food related.

## Convertible Arbitrage

This is an investment strategy that involves taking a long position on a convertible security and a short position in its converting common stock. This strategy attempts to exploit profits when there is a pricing error made in the conversion factor of the convertible security.

## Convertible Bond

A bond that can be exchanged, at the option of the holder, for a specific number of shares of the company's preferred stock or common stock. Convertibility affects the performance of the bond in certain ways. First and foremost, convertible bonds tend to have lower interest rates than nonconvertibles because they also accrue value as the price of the underlying stock rises. In this way, convertible bonds offer some of the benefits of both stocks and bonds. Convertibles earn interest even when the stock is trading down or sideways, but when the stock prices rise, the value of the convertible increases. Therefore, convertibles can offer protection against a decline in stock price. Because they are sold at a premium over the price of the stock, convertibles should be expected to earn that premium back in the first three or four years after purchase.

## Core Fund

Fund that takes a middle of the road approach to generate returns for shareholders. These funds are generally structured in two ways. One strategy is to combine stocks and bonds (and possible income trusts) into a single fund to achieve a steady return and improved asset allocation. The other approach is to combine growth stocks and value stocks to diversify the risk from the typical ups and downs of markets. This type of fund can also be called a blend fund since it can show characteristics of a pure growth fund or a pure value fund. Either way, a core fund is focused to producing long-term results.

## Corporate Bonds

Corporate Bonds are similar to gilts but are a form of borrowing by companies rather than Governments. Let's say Astra Zeneca wished to borrow a billion pounds for research and development. They would initially approach their brokers who would review the strength of Astra Zeneca versus the Government to assess what is a reasonable "risk premium". A secure company might be able to borrow money at 1 or 2 percentage points above the gilt rate and a very insecure company may have to pay 10 percentage points above the Government rate or in some cases substantially more. Companies' security is generally graded from AAA to no rating, the less secure debt being known in the UK as "High Yield", or as it is more accurately described by Americans as "Junk Bonds". So with Corporate Bonds the short term returns will vary in line with interest rates as they do with gilts, but also in line with the perceived strength of the company.

## Correlation

A standardised measure of the relative movement between two variables, such as the price of a fund and an index. The degree of correlation between two variables is measured on a scale of −1 to +1. If two variables move up or down together, they are positively correlated. If they tend to move in opposite directions, they are negatively correlated.

## Coupon

Denotes the rate of interest on a fixed interest security. A 10 % coupon pays interest of 10 % a year on the nominal value of the stock.

## Cyclical Stock

The stock of a company which is sensitive to business cycles and whose performance is strongly tied to the overall economy. Cyclical companies tend to make products or provide services that are in lower demand during downturns in the economy and higher demand during upswings. Examples include the automobile, steel, and housing industries. The stock price of a cyclical company will often rise just before an economic upturn begins and fall just before a downturn begins. Investors in cyclical stocks try to make the largest gains by buying the stock at the bottom of a business cycle, just before a turnaround begins. Opposite of defensive stock.

## D

## Debenture

A loan raised by a company, paying a fixed rate of interest and secured on the assets of the company.

## Defensive Stock

A stock that tends to remain stable under difficult economic conditions. Defensive stocks include food, tobacco, oil, and utilities. These stocks hold up in hard times because demand does not decrease as dramatically as it may in other sectors. Defensive stocks tend to lag behind the rest of the market during economic expansion because demand does not increase as dramatically in an upswing.

## Delta

The rate at which the price of an option changes in response to a move in the price of the underlying security. If an option's delta is 0.5 (out of a maximum of 1), a $2 move in the price of the underlying will produce a $1 move in the option.

*Delta Hedge*
A hedging position that causes a portfolio to be delta neutral.

*Derivatives*
Financial contracts whose value is tied to an underlying asset. Derivatives include futures and options.

*Discount*
When a security is selling below its normal market price, opposite of premium.

*Distressed Securities*
A distressed security is a security of a company which is currently in default, bankruptcy, financial distress or a turnaround situation.

## E

*Efficient Frontier*
A line created from the risk-reward graph, comprised of optimal portfolios. The optimal portfolios plotted along the curve have the highest expected return possible for the given amount of risk.

*EFTA – European Fair-Trade Association*
A network of 11 Fair Trade organisations in nine European countries which import Fair Trade products from some 400 economically disadvantaged producer groups in Africa, Asia and Latin America. EFTA's members are based in Austria, Belgium, France, Germany, Italy, the Netherlands, Spain, Switzerland and the United Kingdom.

*Embedded Value EV*
A method of accounting used by life insurance business. The embedded value is the sum of the net assets of the insurance business under conventional accounting and the present value of the in-force business based on estimates of future cash flows and conservative assumptions about for example, mortality, persistence and expenses. Accounts users prefer this method because it gives a separate indication of new business profitability, a key performance indicator for a life insurer.

*Emerging Markets*
Typically includes markets within countries that have an underdeveloped or developing infrastructure with significant potential for economic growth and increased capital market participation for foreign investors. These countries generally possess some of the following characteristics; per capita GNP less than $9000, recent economic liberalisation, debt ratings below investment grade, recent liberalisation of the political system and non-membership of the Organisation of Economic Cooperation and Development. Because many emerging countries do not allow short selling or offer viable futures or other derivatives products with which to hedge, emerging market investing entails investing in geographic regions that have underdeveloped capital markets and exhibit high growth rates and high rates of inflation. Investing in emerging markets can be very volatile and may also involve currency risk, political risk and liquidity risk. Generally, a long-only investment strategy.

*Emerging Markets Debt*
Debt instruments of emerging market countries. Most bonds are US Dollar denominated and a majority of secondary market trading is in Brady bonds.

*Equities*
Ownership positions in companies that can be traded in public markets. Often produce current income which is paid in the form of quarterly dividends. In the event of the company going bankrupt equity holders' claims are subordinate to the claims of preferred stockholders and bondholders.

*Equity Hedge*
Also known as long / short equity, combines core long holdings of equities with short sales of stock or stock index options. Equity hedge portfolios may be anywhere from net long to net short depending on market conditions. Equity hedge managers generally increase net long exposure in bull markets and decrease net long exposure or are even net short in a bear market.

*Equity Market Neutral*
This investment strategy is designed to exploit equity market inefficiencies and usually involves being simultaneously long and short equity portfolios of the same size within a country. Market neutral portfolios are designed to be either beta or currency neutral or both. Attempts are often made to control industry, sector and market capitalisation exposures.

*Equity Risk*
The risk of owning stock or having some other form of ownership interest.

*Ethical Investing*
Choosing to invest in companies that operate ethically, provide social benefits, and are sensitive to the environment. Also called socially conscious investing.

*EU*
European Union. The economic association of over a dozen European countries which seek to create a unified, barrier-free market for products and services throughout the continent. The majority of countries share a common currency with a unified authority over that currency. Notable exceptions to the common currency are the UK, Sweden, Norway, Denmark.

*Eurobond*
A bond issued and traded outside the country whose currency it is denominated in, and outside the regulations of a single country; usually a bond issued by a non-European company for sale in Europe. Interest is paid gross.

*Eurozone or Euroland*
The collective group of countries which use the Euro as their common currency.

*Event Driven Investing*
Investment strategy seeking to identify and exploit pricing inefficiencies that have been caused by some sort of corporate event such as a merger, spin-off, distressed situation or recapitalisation.

*Exit Fee*

A fee paid to redeem an investment. It is a charge levied for cashing in a fund's capital.

*Exposure*

The condition of being subjected to a source of risk.

**F**

*FCP*

Fonds Commun de Placement. FCPs are a common fund structure in Luxembourg. In contrast to SICAV, they are not companies, but are organised as co-ownerships and must be managed by a fund management company.

*Feeder Fund*

A fund which invests only in another fund. The feeder fund may be a different currency to the main fund and may be used to channel cash in to the main fund for a different currency class.

*Fixed Interest*

The term fixed interest is often used by banks and building societies relating to an account that pays a set rate of interest for a set time period. This type of investment is capital secure and the returns are known at outset. However, fixed interest within the investment world is a completely different concept. It is used to describe funds that invest in Government Gilts and Corporate Bond securities.

*Fixed Income Arbitrage*

Investment strategy that seeks to exploit pricing inefficiencies in fixed income securities and their derivative instruments. Typical investment is long a fixed income security or related instrument that is perceived to be undervalued and short a similar related fixed income security or related instrument. Often highly leveraged.

*Floating Rate*

Any interest rate that changes on a periodic basis. The change is usually tied to movement of an outside indicator, such as the Bank of England Base Rate. Movement above or below certain levels is often prevented by a predetermined floor and ceiling for a given rate. For example, you might see a rate set at "base plus 2%". This means that the rate on the loan will always be 2% higher than the base rate, which changes regularly to take into account changes in the inflation rate. For an individual taking out a loan when rates are low, a fixed rate loan would allow him or her to "lock in" the low rates and not be concerned with fluctuations. On the other hand, if interest rates were historically high at the time of the loan, he or she would benefit from a floating rate loan, because as the prime rate fell to historically normal levels, the rate on the loan would decrease. Also called adjustable rate.

*Floor*
    A contract that protects the holder against a decline in interest rates or prices below a certain point.

*Forward*
    An agreement to execute a transaction at some time in the future. In the foreign exchange market this is a tailor-made deal where an investor agrees to buy or sell an amount of currency at a given date.

*Forward Rate Agreement (FRA)*
    A type of forward contract that is linked to interest rates.

*FTSE 100*
    The Financial Times Stock Exchange 100 stock index, a market cap weighted index of stocks traded on the London Stock Exchange. Similar to the S&P 500 in the United States.

*Fund of Funds*
    An investment vehicle that invests in more than one fund. Portfolio will typically diversify across a variety of investment managers, investment strategies and subcategories. Provides investors with access to managers with higher minimums than individuals might otherwise afford.

*Funds under Management*
   Total amount of funds managed by an entity, excluding

## G

*Gearing*
   The effect that borrowing has on the equity capital of a company or the asset value of a fund. If the assets bought with funds borrowed appreciate in value, the excess of value over funds borrowed will accrue to the shareholder, thus augmenting, or gearing up the value of their investment.

*Geographic Spread*
   The distribution in a fund's portfolio over different parts of the world, either by countries or larger areas.

*Gilt-Edged Securities*
   Stocks and shares issued and guaranteed by the British government to raise funds and traded on the Stock Exchange. A relatively risk-free investment, gilts bear fixed interest and are usually redeemable on a specified date. The term is now used generally to describe securities of the highest value. According to the redemption date, gilts are described as short (up to five years), medium, or long (15 years or more).

*Gilts*
   Gilts are effectively Government borrowing. When the Chancellor does not have sufficient income to meet his expenditure, then the Government will often borrow money in the form of gilts. These can be for a variety of different terms, paying a range of interest rates.

A typical example would be a ten-year gilt which may pay, say, 5% income. This is the most secure investment you could buy, as you know the rate of return and you know when you will receive your capital back. The UK Government has never defaulted on a gilt.

If, however you wanted to access your money before maturity then you would have to sell your gilt on the open market. Let's say you were trying to sell your gilt after one year. In order to obtain a value any potential purchaser will look at the term remaining on your gilt and the interest rate promised and compare this to new gilts being launched at the time. If the Government was then launching a new gilt over a nine-year time period, and promising to pay 6% per annum, then clearly nobody is going to want to pay the same amount of money for your gilt which is offering a lower interest rate.

They would probably therefore offer at least 9% less than you originally paid for it to reflect the 1% difference in income over the nine years of the remaining term. So, whilst you had set out to achieve guaranteed returns, if you sell a gilt before maturity you could potentially make a capital loss on it, in this instance a loss of 9% over
the year.

However, if you decide to keep the gilt until its maturity you will still receive all of your interest and the capital back. Having said this, your valuation each year will vary depending on market conditions.

## GNMA (Ginnie Mae)

Government National Mortgage Association. A U.S. Government-owned agency which buys mortgages from lending institutions, securitizes them, and then sells them to investors. Because the payments to investors are guaranteed by the full faith and credit of the U.S. Government, they return slightly less interest than other mortgage-backed securities.

## Growth Stocks

Stock of a company which is growing earnings and/or revenue faster than its industry or the overall market. Such companies usually pay little or no dividends, preferring to use the income instead to finance further expansion.

## Growth Orientated Portfolios

Dominant theme is growth in revenues, earnings and market share. Many of these portfolios are hedged to mitigate against declines in the overall market.

## Global Macro
The investment strategy is based on shifts in global economies. Derivatives are often used to speculate on currency and interest rate movements.

## Guided Architecture
In relation to funds, for example FPIL Premier policyholders may only go into the FPIL mirror fund range – this is guided architecture. In contrast to FPIL Reserve policyholders who may choose any security – open architecture.


# H

## Hawk
An investor who has a negative view towards inflation and its effects on markets. Hawkish investors prefer higher interest rates in order to maintain reduced inflation.

## Hedge
Any transaction with the objective of limiting exposure to risk such as changes in exchange rates or prices.

## Hedge Fund
A pooled investment vehicle that is privately organised, administered by investment management professionals and generally not widely available to the general public. Many hedge funds share a number of characteristics; they hold long and short positions, use leverage to enhance returns, pay performance or incentive fees to their managers, have high minimum investment requirements and target absolute returns. Generally, hedge funds are not constrained by legal limitations on their investment discretion and can adopt a variety of trading strategies. The hedge fund manager often has its own capital (or that of its principals) invested in the hedge fund it manages.

## Herding
Hedge fund managers while taking a position may encourage other investors to follow this trend.

## High Conviction Stock Picking
A typical portfolio is not constrained by benchmarks, allowing the manager to pursue an approach where a smaller number of stocks are chosen that may bear little or no resemblance to the consensus view. i.e the manager's conviction.

## High Water Mark
The assurance that a fund only takes fees on profits actually earned by an individual investment. For example, a £10 million investment is made in year one and the fund declines by 50%, leaving £5 million in the fund. In year two, the fund returns 100% bringing the investment value back to £10 million. If a fund has a high water mark it will not take incentive fees on the return in year two since the investment has never grown. The fund will only take incentive fees if the investment grows above the initial level of £10 million.

## High-Yield Bond
Often called junk bonds, these are low grade fixed income securities of companies that show significant upside potential. The bond has to pay a high yield due to significant credit risk.

## Hurdle Rate
The minimum investment return a fund must exceed before a performance-based incentive fee can be taken. For example, if a fund has a hurdle rate of 10% and the fund returned 18% for the year, the fund will only take incentive fees on the 8 percentage points above the hurdle rate.

## I

## Index
An arithmetic mean of selected stocks intended to represent the behaviour of the market or some component of it. One example is the FTSE 100 which adds the current prices of the one hundred FTSE 100 stocks and divides the results by a pre-determined number, the divisor.

## Index Funds

A fund that attempts to achieve a performance similar to that stated in an index. The purpose of this fund is to realise an investment return at least equal to the broad market covered by the indices while reducing management costs.

## Index Linked Gilt

A gilt, the interest and capital of which change in line with the Retail Price Index.

## In the Money

A condition where an option has a positive intrinsic value.

## Intrinsic Value

A component of the market value of an option. If the strike price of a call option is cheaper than the prevailing market price, then the option has a positive intrinsic value, and is "in the money".

## Investment Grade

Something classified as investment grade is, by implication, medium to high quality.

1) In the case of a stock, a firm that has a strong balance sheet, considerable capitalisation and is recognized as a leader in its industry.
2) In the case of fixed income, a bond with a rating of BBB or higher.

## J

## January Effect

Tendency of US stock markets to rise between December 31 and the end of the first week in January. The January Effect occurs because many investors choose to sell some of their stock right before the end of the year in order to claim a capital loss for tax purposes. Once the tax calendar rolls over to a new year on January 1st these same investors quickly reinvest their money in the market, causing stock prices to rise. Although the January Effect has been observed numerous times throughout history, it is difficult for investors to profit from it since the market as a whole expects it to happen and therefore adjusts its prices accordingly.

*Junk Bond*
A bond that pays a high yield due to significant credit risk

## L

*Leverage*
When investors borrow funds to increase the amount they have invested in a particular position, they use leverage. Sometimes managers use leverage to enable them to put on new positions without having to take off other positions prematurely. Managers who target very small price discrepancies or spreads will often use leverage to magnify the returns from these discrepancies. Leverage both magnifies the risk of the strategy as well as creates risk by giving the lender power over the disposition of the investment portfolio. This may occur in the form of increased margin requirements or adverse market shifts, forcing a partial or complete liquidation of the portfolio.

The amount of leverage used by the fund is commonly expressed as a percentage of the fund. For example, if the fund has £1 million and borrows another £2 million to bring the total invested to £3 million, then the fund is leveraged 200%

*Life Cycle Funds*
Life-cycle funds are the closest thing the industry has to a maintenance-free retirement fund. Life-cycle funds, also referred to as "age-based funds" or "target-date funds", are a special breed of the balanced fund. They are a type of fund of funds structured between equity and fixed income. But the distinguishing feature of the life-cycle fund is that its overall asset allocation automatically adjusts to become more conservative as your expected retirement date approaches. While life-cycle funds have been around for a while, they have been gaining popularity.

*LIBOR*
London Inter Bank Offered Rate.

*Liquidity*
1) The degree to which an asset or security can be bought or sold in the market without affecting the asset's price. Liquidity is characterized by a high level of trading activity.
2) The ability to convert an asset to cash quickly.
Investing in illiquid assets is riskier because there might not be a way for you to get your money out of the investment. Examples of assets with good liquidity include blue chip common stock and those assets in the money market. A fund with good liquidity would be characterised by having enough units outstanding to allow large transactions without a substantial change in price.

*Liquidity Risk*
Risk from a lack of liquidity, ie an investor having difficulty getting their money out of an investment.

*Listed Security*
Stock or bond that has been accepted for trading by an organised and registered securities exchange. Advantages of being listed are an orderly market place, more liquidity, fair price determination, accurate and continuous reporting on sales and quotations, information on listed companies and strict regulations for the protection of securities holders.

*Lock Up / Lock In*
Time period during which an initial investment cannot be redeemed.

*Long Position*
Holding a positive amount of an asset (or an asset underlying a derivative instrument)

*Long / Short Hedged*
Also described as the Jones Model. Manager buys securities he believes will go up in price and sells short securities he believes will decline in price. Manager will be either net long or net short and may change the net position frequently. For example, a manager may be

60% long and 100% short, giving him a market exposure of 40% net short. The basic belief behind this strategy is that it will enhance the manager's stock picking ability and protect investors in all market conditions.

## M

*Macro-Economics*

The field of economics that studies the behaviour of the economy as a whole. Macroeconomics looks at economy-wide phenomena such as changes in unemployment, national income, rate of growth, and price levels.

*Managed Accounts*

Accounts of individual investors which are managed individually by an investment manager. The minimum size is usually in excess of £3 million.

*Managed Futures*

An approach to fund management that uses positions in government securities, futures contracts, options on futures contracts and foreign exchange in a portfolio. Some managers specialise in physical commodity futures but most find they must trade a variety of financial and non-financial contracts if they have considerable assets under management.

*Management Fee*

The fees taken by the manager on the entire asset level of the investment. For example, if at the end of the period the investment is valued at £1 million and the management fee is 1.2%, then the fee would be £12,000.

*Margin*

The amount of assets that must be deposited in a margin account in order to secure a portion of a party's obligations under a contract. For example, to buy or sell an exchange traded futures contract, a party must post a specified amount that is determined by the exchange, referred to as initial margin. In addition, a party will be required to post variation margin if the futures contracts change in value. Margin is also required in connection with the purchase and sale of securities where the full purchase price is not paid up front or the securities sold are not owned by the seller.

*Market Maker*
An Exchange member firm that is obliged to make a continuous two-way price, that is to offer to buy and sell securities in which it is registered throughout the mandatory quote period.

*Market Neutral Investing*
An investment strategy that aims to produce almost the same profit regardless of market circumstances, often by taking a combination of long and short positions. This approach relies on the manager's ability to make money through relative valuation analysis, rather than through market direction forecasting. The strategy attempts to eliminate market risk and be profitable in any market condition.

*Market Risk*
Risk from changes in market prices

*Market Timing*
1) An accepted practice of allocating assets among investments by switching into investments that appear to be beginning an up trend, and switching out of investments that appear to be starting a downtrend.
2) An increasingly unacceptable / illegal practice of undertaking frequent or large transactions in mutual funds. Especially where there is a time difference between the close of the relevant markets that the fund invests in and the valuation of the fund. ie a Far East fund that is valued the next day in the UK.

*Market Value*
The value at which an asset trades or would trade in the market.

*Mark to Market*
When the value of securities in a portfolio are updated to reflect the changes that have occurred due to the movement of the

underlying market. The security will then be valued at its current market price.

*Maximum Draw Down*
    The largest loss suffered by a security or fund, peak to trough, over a given period, usually one month.

*Merger Arbitrage*
    Sometimes called Risk Arbitrage, involves investment in event-driven situations such as leveraged buy outs, mergers and hostile takeovers. Normally the stock of an acquisition target appreciates while the acquiring company's stock decreases in value.

*Mezzanine Level*
    Stage of a company's development just prior to its going public. Venture capitalists entering at that point have a lower risk of loss than at previous stages and can look forward to early capital appreciation as a result of the market value gained by an initial public offering.

*Micro-Economics*
    The behaviour and purchasing decisions of individuals and firms.

*Money Market Funds*
    Mutual funds that invest in short term highly liquid money market instruments. These funds are used when preservation of capital is paramount. They may be used to "park" money between investments, especially during periods of market uncertainty.

*Mortgage Backed Security*
    A pass-through security that aggregates a pool of mortgage-backed debt obligations. Mortgage-backed securities' principal amounts are usually government guaranteed. Homeowners' principal and interest payments pass from the originating bank through a government agency or investment bank, to investors, net of a loan servicing fee payable to the originator.

## Multi-Manager Product

An investment pool that allocates assets to a number of managers with different investment styles. This methodology facilitates a high degree of diversification and accordingly the potential for a greater spread of risk. Hedge funds often have this structure. Smaller investors are able to enjoy access to a greater variety of managers that would normally be prohibited by minimum investment requirements for each manager. Funds of funds are a classic multi-manager product.

## Municipal Bond (USA)

A debt security issued by a state, municipality, or county, in order to finance its capital expenditures. Municipal bonds are exempt from federal taxes and from most state and local taxes, especially if you live in the state the bond is issued. Such expenditures might include the construction of highways, bridges or schools. "Munis" are bought for their favourable tax implications and are popular with people
in high income tax brackets.

## Mutual Fund

A security that gives small investors access to a well diversified portfolio of equities, bonds, and other securities. Each shareholder participates in the gain or loss of the fund. Shares are issued and can be redeemed as needed. The fund's net asset value (NAV) is determined each day. Each mutual fund portfolio is invested to match the objective stated in the prospectus. Some examples of mutual funds are UK Unit Trusts, Open-ended Investment Companies (OEICs), EU registered UCITS, Luzembourg based SICAVs.

## N

## NAREIT

National Association of Real Estate Investment Trusts

## Nasdaq

A computerised system established by the NASD to facilitate trading by providing broker/dealers with current bid and ask price quotes on over-the-counter stocks and some listed stocks. Unlike the Amex and the NYSE, the Nasdaq (once an acronym for the National Association of securities Dealers Automated Quotation system) does not have a physical trading floor that brings together buyers and sellers. Instead, all trading on the Nasdaq exchange is done over a network of computers and telephones. Also, the Nasdaq does not employ market specialists to buy unfilled orders like the NYSE does. The Nasdaq began when brokers started informally trading via telephone; the network was later formalized and linked by computer in the early 1970s. In 1998 the parent company of the Nasdaq purchased the Amex, although the two continue to operate separately. Orders for stock are sent out electronically on the Nasdaq, where market makers list their buy and sell prices. Once a price is agreed upon, the transaction is executed electronically.

## Net Asset Value (NAV)
NAV equals the closing market value of all assets within a portfolio after subtracting all liabilities including accrued fees and expenses. NAV per share is the NAV divided by the number of shares in issue. This is often used as the price of a fund. A purchase fee may be added to the NAV when buying units in the fund. This fee is typically 1-7%.

## Net Exposure
The exposure level of a fund to the market. It is calculated by subtracting the short percentage from the long percentage. For example if a fund is 100% long and 30% short, then the net exposure is 70% long.

## Nominee Name
Name in which a security is registered and held in trust on behalf of the beneficial owner.

# O

## Offer Price
The price at which a fund manager or market maker will sell shares to you. (ie offer them to you). The offer price is higher than the Bid Price which is the price at which they will buy shares from

you. (ie they will make a bid). This is one way in which a market maker turns a profit. A fund manager may use the difference to cover dealing administration costs.

*Offshore*
Located or based outside of one's national boundaries. Typically, these locations have preferential tax treatments and fund legislation.

*Open Architecture*
In relation to funds, for example FPIL Reserve policyholders may choose any security – open architecture. In contrast to FPIL Premier policyholders who may only go into the FPIL mirror fund range – this is guided architecture.

*Open-ended Funds*
These are funds where units or shares can be bought and sold daily and where the number of units or shares in issue can vary daily.

*Opportunistic Investing*
A general term describing any fund that is opportunistic in nature. These types of funds are usually aggressive and seek to make money in the most efficient way at any given time. Investment themes are dominated by events that are seen as special situations or short-term opportunities to capitalise from price fluctuations or imbalances, such as initial public offering.

*Option*
A privilege sold by one party to another that offers the buyer the right, but not the obligation, to buy (call)or sell (put) a security at an agreed-upon price during a certain period of time or on a specific date. Options are extremely versatile securities that can be used in many different ways. Traders use optionsto speculate, which is a relatively risky practice, while hedgers use options to reduce the risk of holding an asset.

*Over the Counter- OTC*
A security traded in some context other than on a formal exchange such as the LSE, NYSE, DJIA, TSX, AMEX, etc. A stock is traded over the counter usually because the company is small and

unable to meet listing requirements of the exchanges. Also known as unlisted stock, these securities are traded by brokers/dealers who negotiate directly with one another over computer networks and by phone. The Nasdaq, however, is also considered to be an OTC market, with the tier 1 being represented by companies such as Microsoft, Dell and Intel. Instruments such as bonds do not trade on a formal exchange and are thus considered over-the- counter securities. Most debt instruments are traded by investment banks making markets for specific issues. If someone wants to buy or sell a bond, they call the bank that makes the market in that bond and ask for quotes. Many derivative instruments such as forwards, swaps and most exotic derivatives are also traded OTC.

*Out of the Money*
   This refers to options:
   1) For a call, when an option's strike price is higher than the market price of the underlying stock.
   2) For a put, when the strike price is below the market price of the underlying stock.
   Basically, an option that would be worthless if it expired today.

*Over-Hedging*
   Locking in a price, such as through a futures contract, for more goods, commodities or securities that is required to protect a position. While hedging does protect a position, over-hedging can be costly in the form of missed opportunities. Although you can lock in a selling price, over-hedging might result in a producer or seller missing out on favourable market prices. For example, if you entered into a January futures contract to sell 25,000 shares of 'Smith Holdings' at $6.50 per share you would not be able to take advantage if the spot price jumped to $7.00.

*Overlay Strategy*
   A type of derivatives strategy. This strategy is often employed to provide protection from currencies or interest rate movements that are not the primary focus of the main portfolio strategy.

## Overweight

Refers to an investment position that is larger than the generally accepted benchmark. For example, if a company normally holds a portfolio whose weighting of cash is 10%, and then increases cash holdings to 15%, the portfolio would have an overweight position in cash.

## P

### Pair Trading

The strategy of matching a long position with a short position in two stocks of the same sector. This creates a hedge against the sector and the overall market that the two stocks are in. The hedge createdis essentially a bet that you are placing on the two stocks; the stock you are long in versus the stock you are short in. It's the ultimate strategy for stock pickers, because stock picking is all that counts. What the actual market does won't matter (much). If the market or the sector moves in one direction or the other, the gain on the long stock is offset by a loss on the short.

### Percent Long

The percentage of a fund invested in long positions.

### Percent Short

The percentage of a fund that is sold short.

### Performance Fee

The fee payable to the fund adviser on new profits earned by the fund for the period.

### Portfolio Turnover

The number of times an average portfolio security is replaced during an accounting period, usually a year.

### Premium

The total cost of an option. The premium of an option is basically the sum of the option's intrinsic and time value. It is important to note that volatility also affects the premium.

The difference between the higher price paid for a fixed-income security and the security's face amount at issue. If a fixed-income security (bond) is purchased at a premium, existing interest rates are lower than the coupon rate. Investors pay a premium for an investment that will return an amount greater than existing interest rates.

*Price Earnings Ratio (P/E Ratio)*
A valuation ratio of a company's current share price compared to its per-share earnings. Calculated as: Market Value per Share/Earnings per Share (EPS)

EPS is usually from the last four quarters (trailing P/E), but sometimes can be taken from the estimates of earnings expected in the next four quarters (projected or forward P/E). A third variation is the sum of the last two actual quarters and the estimates of the next two quarters.

Sometimes the P/E is referred to as the "multiple," because it shows how much investors are willing to pay per dollar of earnings. In general, a high P/E means high projected earnings in the future. However, the P/E ratio actually doesn't tell us a whole lot by itself. It's usually only useful to compare the P/E ratios of companies in the same industry, or to the market in general, or against the company's own historical P/E.

*Prime Broker*
A broker which acts as settlement agent, provides custody for assets, provides financing for leverage, and prepares daily account statements for its clients, who might be money managers, hedge funds, market makers, arbitrageurs, specialists and other professional investors.

*Private Placement / Private Equity*
When equity capital is made available to companies or investors, but not quoted on a stock market. The funds raised through private equity can be used to develop new products and technologies, to expand working capital, to make acquisitions, or to strengthen a company's balance sheet. The average individual investor will not

have access to private equity because it requires a very large investment. The result is the sale of securities to a relatively small number of investors. Private placements do not have to be registered with organizations such as the FSA, SEC because no public offering is involved.

## Proprietary Trading

When a firm trades for direct gain instead of commission dollars. Essentially, the firm has decided to profit from the market rather than commissions from processing trades. Firms who engage in proprietary trading believe they have a competitive advantage that will enable them to earn excess returns.

## Prospectus

In the case of mutual funds, a prospectus describes the fund's objectives, history, manager background, and financial statements. A prospectus makes investors aware of the risks of an investment and in most jurisdictions is required to be published by law.

## Protected Cell Company

A standard limited company that has been separated into legally distinct portions or cells. The revenue streams, assets and liabilities of each cell are kept separate from all other cells. Each cell has its own separate portion of the PCC's overall share capital, allowing shareholders to maintain sole ownership of an entire cell while owning only a small proportion of the PCC as a whole. PCCs can provide a means of entry into a captive insurance market to entities for which it was previously uneconomic. The overheads of a protected cell captive can be shared between the owners of each of the cells, making the captive cheaper to run from the point of view of the insured.

## Purification

The process whereby Muslims give to charity any interest deemed to have been credited to their holdings in funds or stocks.

*Put Option*
   An option giving the holder the right, but not the obligation, to sell a specific quantity of an asset for a fixed price during a specific period.

## Q

*Qualitative Analysis*
   Analysis that uses subjective judgment in evaluating securities based on non-financial information such as management expertise, cyclicality of industry, strength of research and development, and labour relations.

*Quantitative Analysis*
   A security analysis that uses financial information derived from company annual reports and income statements to evaluate an investment decision. Some examples are financial ratios, the cost of capital, asset valuation, and sales and earnings trends.

*Quasi Sovereign Bond*
   Debt issued by a public sector entity that is, like a sovereign bond, guaranteed by the sovereign, however there is a difference in that there may be a timing difference in repayment in the unlikely event of default.

## R

*REIT Real Estate Investment Trust*
   A security that trades like a stock on the major exchanges and invests in real estate directly, through either properties or mortgages.

REITs receive special tax considerations and typically offer investors high yields, as well as a highly liquid method of investing in real estate. Equity REITs invest in and own properties (thus responsible for the equity or value of their real estate assets). Their revenues come principally from their properties' rents. Mortgage REITs deal in investment and ownership of property mortgages. These REITs loan money for mortgages to owners of real estate, or purchase existing mortgages or mortgage-backed securities. Their revenues are generated primarily by the interest that they earn on the mortgage loans. Hybrid REITs combine the investment strategies of equity REITs and mortgage REITs by investing in both properties and mortgages.

## R – Squared

A statistical measure that represents the percentage of a fund's or security's movements that are explained by movements in a benchmark index. It is a measure of correlation with the benchmark. R-squared values range from 0 to 100. An R-squared of 100 means that all movements of a security are completely explained by movements in the index. ie perfect correlation.

## Repurchase Agreement (Repo)

A form of short-term borrowing for dealers in government securities. The dealer sells the government securities to investors, usually on an overnight basis, and buys them back the following day. For the party selling the security (and agreeing to repurchase it in the future) it is a repo; for the party on the other end of the transaction (buying the security and agreeing to sell in the future) it is a reverse repurchase agreement. Repos are classified as a money-market instrument. They are usually used to raise short-term capital.

## Risk Adjusted Rate of Return

A measure of how much risk a fund or portfolio took on to earn its returns, usually expressed as a number or a rating. This is often represented by the Sharpe Ratio. The more return per unit of risk, the better

## Risk Arbitrage

A broad definition for three types of arbitrage that contain an element of risk:
1) Merger and Acquisition Arbitrage - The simultaneous purchase of stock in a company being acquired and the sale (or short sale) of stock in the acquiring company.

2) Liquidation Arbitrage - The exploitation of a difference between a company's current value and its estimated liquidation value.

3) Pairs Trading - The exploitation of a difference between two very similar companies in the same industry that have historically been highly correlated. When the two company's values diverge to a historically high level you can take an offsetting position in each (e.g. go long in one and short the other) because, as history has shown, they will inevitably come to be similarly valued.

In theory true arbitrage is riskless, however, the world in which we operate offers very few of these opportunities. Despite these forms of arbitrage being somewhat risky, they are still relatively low-risk trading strategies which money managers (mainly hedge fund managers) and retail investors alike can employ.

## Risk-Free Rate

The quoted rate on an asset that has virtually no risk. The rate quoted for US treasury bills are widely used as the risk-free rate.

## Risk Reward Ratio

This is closely related to the Sharpe Ratio, except the risk reward ratio does not use a risk-free rate in its calculation. The higher the risk reward ratio, the better. Calculated as: Annualised rate of return/Annualised Standard Deviation

## S

## Santa Claus Rally

The rise in US stock prices that sometimes occurs in the week after Christmas, often in anticipation of the January effect.

## Satellite Fund

Specialist mandate fund that offers greater breadth of proposition than a "core" fund.

## Secondary Market

A market in which an investor purchases an asset from another investor, rather than an issuing corporation. A good example is the London Stock Exchange. All stock exchanges are part of the secondary market, as investors buy securities from other investors instead of an issuing company.

## Sector Fund

A mutual fund whose objective is to invest in a particular industry or sector of the economy to capitalize on returns. Because most of the stocks in this type of fund are all in the same industry, there is a lack of diversification. The fund tends to do very well or not well at all, depending on the conditions of the specific sector.

## Securities

General name for all stocks and shares of all types.

## Securities Lending

When a brokerage lends securities owned by its clients to short sellers. This allows brokers to create additional revenue (commissions) on the short sale transaction.

## Semi-gilt

A financial instrument through which a municipality or parastatal (owned or controlled wholly or partly by the government) borrows money from the public in exchange for a fixed repayment plan.

## SICAV

SICAV stands for Societe D'Investissement a Capital Variable. It is a Luxembourg incorporated company that is responsible for the management of a mutual fund and manages a portfolio of securities. The share capital is equal to the net assets of the fund. The units in the portfolio are delivered as shares and the investors are referred to as shareholders. SICAVs are common fund structures in Luxembourg.

## Sharia(h)

Sharia refers to the body of Islamic law. The term means "way" or "path"; it is the legal framework within which public and some private aspects of life are regulated for those living in a legal system based on Muslim principles.

*Sharpe Ratio*
A ratio developed by Bill Sharpe to measure risk-adjusted performance. It is calculated by subtracting the risk-free rate from the rate of return for a portfolio and dividing the result by the standard deviation of the portfolio returns.

Calculated as: Expected Portfolio Return – Risk Free Rate/Portfolio Standard Deviation

The Sharpe ratio tells us whether the returns of a portfolio are because of smart investment decisions or a result of excess risk. The Sortino Ratio is a variation of this.

*Short Selling*
The selling of a security that the seller does not own, or any sale that is completed by the delivery of a security borrowed by the seller. Short sellers assume that they will be able to buy the stock at a lower amount than the price at which they sold short. Selling short is the opposite of going long. That is, short sellers make money if the stock goes down in price. This is an advanced trading strategy with many unique risks and pitfalls.

*Small Caps*
Stocks or funds with smaller capitalisation. They tend to be less liquid than blue chips, but they tend to have higher returns.

*Soft Commissions*
A means of paying brokerage firms for their services through commission revenue, as opposed to normal payments. For example, a mutual fund may offer to pay for the research of a brokerage firm by executing trades at the brokerage.

*Sovereign Debt*
A debt instrument guaranteed by a government.

Special Situations Investing
Strategy that seeks to profit from pricing discrepancies resulting from corporate event transactions such as mergers and acquisitions,

spin-offs, bankruptcies or recapitalisations. Type of event-driven strategy.

*Specific Risk*
Risk that affects a very small number of assets. This is sometimes referred to as "unsystematic risk." An example would be news that is specific to either one stock or a small number of stocks, such as a sudden strike by the employees of a company you have shares in or a new governmental regulation affecting a particular group of companies. Unlike systematic risk or market risk, specific risk can be diversified away.

*Spin Off*
A new, independant company created through selling or distributing new shares for an existing part of another company. Spinoffs may be done through a rights offering.

*Sponsors*
Lead investors in a fund who supply the seed money. Often the general partner in a hedge fund.

*Spread*
1) The difference between the bid and the offer prices of a security or asset.
2) An options position established by purchasing one option and selling another option of the same class, but of a different series

*Standard Deviation*
Tells us how much the return on the fund is deviating from the expected normal returns.

*Stop-Loss Order*
An order placed with a broker to sell a security when it reaches a certain price. It is designed to limit an investor's loss on a security position. This is sometimes called a "stop market order." In other words, setting a stop-loss order for 10% below the price you paid for the stock would limit your loss to 10%.

*Strategic Bond Funds*
Invest primarily in higher yielding assets including high yield bonds, investment grade bonds, preference shares and other bonds. The funds take strategic asset allocation decisions between countries, asset classes, sectors and credit ratings.

*Strike Price*
The stated price per share for which underlying stock may be purchased (for a call) or sold (for a put) by the option holder upon exercise of the option contract.

*Swap*
Traditionally, the exchange of one security for another to change the maturity (bonds), quality of issues (stocks or bonds), or because investment objectives have changed. Recently, swaps have grown to include currency swaps and interest rates swaps. If firms in separate countries have comparative advantages on interest rates, then a swap could benefit both firms. For example, one firm may have a lower fixed interest rate, while another has access to a lower floating interest rate. These firms could swap to take advantage of the lower rates.

*Swaption (Swap Option)*
The option to enter into an interest rate swap. In exchange for an option premium, the buyer gains the right but not the obligation to enter into a specified swap agreement with the issuer on a specified future date.

*Swing Trading (Swings)*
A style of trading that attempts to capture gains in a stock within one to four days. To find situations in which a stock has this extraordinary potential to move in such a short time frame, the trader must act quickly. This is mainly used by at-home and day traders. Large institutions trade in sizes too big to move in and out of stocks quickly. The individual trader is able to exploit the short-term stock movements without the competition of major traders. Swing traders use technical analysis to look for stocks with short-term price

momentum. These traders aren't interested in the fundamental or intrinsic value of stocks but rather in their price trends and patterns.

### Systematic Risk

The risk inherent to the entire market or entire market segment. Also known as "un-diversifiable risk" or "market risk." interest rates, recession and wars all represent sources of systematic risk because they will affect the entire market and cannot be avoided through diversification. Whereas this type of risk affects a broad range of securities, unsystematic risk affects a very specific group of securities or an individual security. Systematic risk can be mitigated only by being hedged.

### Systemic Risk
Risk that threatens an entire financial system.

### S&P500
Standard & Poor's Index of the New York Stock Exchange. A basket of 500 stocks that are considered to be widely held. The S&P 500 index is weighted by market value, and its performance is thought to be representative of the stock market as a whole.

### T

### Treasury Bill
A negotiable debt obligation issued by the U.S. government and backed by its full faith and credit, having a maturity of one year or less. Exempt from state and local taxes. Also called Bill or T-Bill or U.S. Treasury Bill.

### Time Value
The amount by which an option's premium exceeds its intrinsic value. Also called time premium.

### Top-Down Investing
An investment strategy which first finds the best sectors or industries to invest in, and then searches for the best companies within those sectors or industries. This investing strategy begins with

a look at the overall economic picture and then narrows it down to sectors, industries and companies that are expected to perform well. Analysis of the fundamentals of a given security is the final step.

*Tracking Error*

This statistic measures the standard deviation of a fund's excess returns over the returns of an index or benchmark portfolio. As such, it can be an indication of 'riskiness' in the manager's investment style. A Tracking Error below 2 suggests a passive approach, with a close fit between the fund and its benchmark. At 3 and above the correlation is progressively looser: the manager will be deploying a more active investment style and taking bigger positions away from the benchmark's composition.

*Traded Endowment Policy - TEP*

An Endowment Policy is a type of life insurance that has a value that is payable to the insured if he/she is still living on the policy's maturity date, or to a beneficiary otherwise. They are normally "with profits policies". If the insured does not wish to wait until maturity to receive the value, they can either surrender it back to the issuing insurance company, or they can sell the policy on the open market. If the policy is sold it then becomes a Traded Endowment Policy or TEP. TEP Funds aim to buy and sell TEPs at advantageous prices to make a profit.

*Traded Options*

Transferable options with the right to buy or sell a standardised amount of a security at a fixed price within a specified period.

*Traditional Investments*

Includes equities, bonds, high yield bonds, emerging markets debt, cash, cash equivalents.

## *U*

*Umbrella Fund*

An investment company which has a group of sub-funds (pools) each having its own investment portfolio. The purpose of this structure is to provide investment flexibility and widen investor choice.

## Underlier or Underlying Security

A security or commodity, which is subject to delivery upon exercise of an option contract or convertible security. Exceptions include index options and futures, which cannot be delivered and are therefore settled in cash.

## Underweight

A situation where a portfolio does not hold a sufficient amount of securities to satisfy the accepted benchmark of the portfolio's asset allocation strategy. For example, if a portfolio normally holds 40% stock and currently holds 30%, the position in equities would be considered underweight.

## Unit Trust

A common form of collective investment (similar to a mutual fund) where investors' money is pooled and invested into a variety of shares and bonds in order to reduce risk. Its capital structure is open ended as units can be created or redeemed depending on demand from investors. It should be noted that a Unit Trust means something completely different in the US.

## V

## Value of New Business VNB

Sum of all income (i.e. charges) from new policies minus costs of setting up the policies (i.e. commission) discounted to present day value.

## Value Stocks

Stocks which are perceived to be selling at a discount to their intrinsic or potential worth, i.e. undervalued; or stocks which are out of favour with the market and are under-followed by analysts. It is believed that the share price of these stocks will increase as the value of the company is recognised by the market.

*Value-Added Monthly Index (VAMI)*

An index that tracks the monthly performance of a hypothetical $1000 investment. The calculation for the current month's VAMI is: Previous VAMI x (1 + Current Rate of Return)

The value-added monthly index charts the total return gained by an investor from reinvestment of any dividends and additional interest gained through compounding. The VAMI index is sometimes used to evaluate the performance of a fund manager.

*Venture Capital*

Money and resources made available to start-up firms and small businesses with exceptional growth potential. Venture capital often also includes managerial and technical expertise. Most venture capital money comes from an organized group of wealthy investors who seek substantially above average returns and who are willing to accept correspondingly high risks. This form of raising capital is increasingly popular among new companies that, because of a limited operating history, can't raise money through a debt issue. The downside for entrepreneurs is that venture capitalists usually receive a say in the major decisions of the company in addition to a portion of the equity.

*Volatility*

Standard deviation is a statistical measurement which, when applied to an investment fund, expresses its volatility, or risk. It shows how widely a range of returns varied from the fund's average return over a particular period. Low volatility reduces the risk of buying into an investment in the upper range of its deviation cycle, then seeing its value head towards the lower extreme. For example, if a fund had an average return of 5%, and its volatility was 15, this would mean that the range of its returns over the period had swung between +20% and -10%. Another fund with the same average return and 5% volatility would return between 10% and nothing, but there would at least be no loss.

38838225R00063

Printed in Poland
by Amazon Fulfillment
Poland Sp. z o.o., Wrocław